MAGICAL MEETINGS

No Matter Who Is In The Room

"*Like having coffee with an expert*"

ALSO BY DOUGLAS FERGUSON

Beyond The Prototype

Start Within

How To Remix Anything

ALSO BY JOHN FITCH

Time Off

How To Remix Anything

MAGICAL MEETINGS

No Matter Who Is In The Room

IDEAPRESS
PUBLISHING

BY DOUGLAS FERGUSON
& JOHN FITCH

IDEAPRESS
PUBLISHING

Published in the United States by Ideapress Publishing.

All trademarks are the property of their respective companies.

Cover Design by Victoria Kim

Cataloging-in-Publication Data is on file with the Library of Congress.

ISBN: 978-1-64687-026-4

Special Sales
Ideapress Books are available at a special discount for bulk
purchases for sales promotions and premiums, or for use
in corporate training programs. Special editions, including
personalized covers, a custom foreword, corporate imprints, and
bonus content are also available.

Non-Obvious® is a registered trademark of the Influential
Marketing Group.

DEDICATION

To those who hold space and facilitate magical meetings that
demonstrate no single person is smarter, more capable, or more
creative than an entire room.

Meetings suck, but they don't have to. Read this book to learn how to improve your in-person (or virtual) meeting facilitation skills, inspire more collaboration, and transform any business gathering to be just a little more magical.

PUBLISHER'S NOTE

Is This Guide for You?

If you picked up this book, you are not a dummy.

Many business guides treat you like an idiot. Some even say so on the cover. This is not one of those books.

The Non-Obvious Guides all focus on sharing advice that you haven't heard before. In this guide, you will learn what it takes to create, moderate and participate in better meetings - in-person or virtually.

Asking Douglas and John to author this book was an easy choice. Their approach to making meetings magical is useful, effective and yes, non-obvious.

So read this book, use these insights and transform the way you collaborate with people in any room.

ROHIT BHARGAVA
Founder, Non-Obvious Guides

PART 3—AFTER YOUR MEETINGS AND YOUR MEETING CULTURE

How to Read This Book

Throughout this book you will find links to helpful guides and resources online.

> **FOR ONLINE RESOURCES, VISIT**
> https://www.magicalmeetings.com

Referenced in the book, you will also see these symbols that refer to content to further your learning.

FOLLOW THE ICONS

TEMPLATES
One-page templates to help you strategize

DOWNLOADS
Excerpts or useful further reading

TUTORIALS
Detailed lessons on how to do a task

VIDEOS
Videos to watch online

CHAPTER SUMMARY
Key takeaways and important points

In this book, you will learn to transform your culture so you can ...

- ✔ Prevent terrible meetings from happening.

- ✔ Optimize agendas with the use of narratives.

- ✔ Handpick effective meeting exercises to better engage participants.

- ✔ Maintain momentum outside of your meetings and ensure things get done.

- ✔ Distinguish between work that should be done in a meeting and work that shouldn't.

- ✔ Make meetings more playful, productive, and (yes) magical.

- ✔ Unleash the potential in everyone so that you can all do your best work together, but also alone.

Introduction

DOES FACILITATION EVEN MATTER ANYMORE?

At the start of 2020, we hosted a summit for professional facilitators to learn from each other and level up their abilities to host magical meetings—the kind of meetings where participants feel like there was real progress and connection. Hundreds of us gathered to share our magical meeting approaches.

Little did we know that almost a month later, our entire world would change.

We were facilitating a meeting with community leaders to think about the South by Southwest (SXSW) conference and discuss how the tech community could get together and be proactive about limiting the spread of a new virus called COVID-19. We were meeting to take the best of technology and make it a safer global conference.

Our workshop empowered participants to prototype answers to:

→ How could we practice social distancing at the conference?

→ What are ways we could use artificial intelligence (AI) to recognize whether someone had a fever?

→ Could we offer tests to badge-holders?

In the middle of prototyping solutions and socializing ideas, our workshop was interrupted by a big surprise: The City of Austin decided to cancel SXSW. For many of us in the room, that was the moment we realized we were dealing with a global pandemic.

As we write this book, the pandemic is still forcing us to remain isolated. Optimists see it as a great reset, and pessimists see it as the beginning of the end.

Regardless, we need more human connection, equality, transcendent leadership, and enormous paradigm shifts to occur before any of us feel comfortable again.

We can't do it alone; we still need to meet and create change.

One thing is for sure: If the art of effective meetings was important before, it has become even more essential during this global pandemic and the other cultural challenges we face.

As a result of the shift to distributed workforces, the total amount of our time spent in meetings is increasing. Adapting to all of this as professional meeting facilitators and helping train up leaders and managers has shown us that in order to have culture-changing ideas and outcomes, we need to improve the way we meet together.

And now that we are all facilitators in some capacity, we need to answer big questions:

→ How are we going to better prepare for future pandemics?

→ What do more abundant and equitable societies look like?

→ How do we foster more ethical leadership worldwide?

→ How do we properly incentivize entrepreneurship so that more people create value in our world?

→ What kind of economic and environmental situation is the next generation going to be handed?

As Carl Sagan said, "Our posturings, our imagined self-importance, the delusion that we have some privileged position in the Universe, are challenged by this point of pale light. Our planet is a lonely speck in the great enveloping cosmic dark. In our obscurity, in all this vastness, there is no hint that help will come from elsewhere to save us from ourselves."[1]

Sagan is correct: We must answer these big questions ourselves. Not alone, but as collectives and teams.

Adopting a magical meetings facilitation mindset can help you unlock the potential in any room filled with any kind of participants. It is a superpower for navigating the challenges and opportunities of tomorrow.

What if you could enable all meetings to be purposeful, participatory, principled, and playful?

What if you helped empower the creator and collaborator in everyone you work with?

What if you could host meetings that will not only change you, but change the world?

You can. This guide will be your playbook for doing it.

WHAT IS A MAGICAL MEETING?

If a meeting was magical, everyone who participated feels like they didn't waste their time. They don't regret participating in the meeting because they found it useful.

Making participants feel that the meeting was worthwhile is a facilitator's responsibility. To properly facilitate means to make things easier for everyone else.

All of us are likely to eventually facilitate a meeting. And if you never do, the advice in this guide will still help you—to become an even better meeting participant.

As two people who have coached many companies to create more magical meeting cultures, we must hold ourselves accountable to these standards as well. We designed our own meeting mantras to help lead magical meetings.

Here are our favorites for your inspiration:

The Ten Meeting Mantras

✓ No Purpose, No Meeting

✓ Disagree & Commit

✓ Bring Your Best Self

✓ Do the Work in the Meeting

✓ Foster Emotional Safety

✓ Capture Room Intelligence

✓ Embrace the Child's Mind

✓ Respect Everyone's Time

✓ Decide What Not to Do

✓ Debrief for Durability

The rest of this guide helps you embody the spirit of these mantras. Even if you currently practice all of them in your meetings, you will still pick up on the advanced details in the remaining pages.

Let's consider one of the mantras: "Do the Work in the Meeting." Adopting this mantra helps everyone leave a meeting with a sense of accomplishment because good work was done in the meeting.

But meetings come in different forms, so let's apply this mantra to different types of meetings we experience and examine how that advice plays out.

FOUR TYPES OF MEETINGS

→ **Magical Workshop:** We generate ideas/artifacts with a diverse group of people, we make sense of all the assets and visual creations; we prioritize and decide what to continue making; everyone has a clear path forward.

→ **Magical Sales Meeting:** We meet to understand the needs of a potential customer. We ask great questions and listen. We give a demonstration of what we can do. Our product/service is either an obvious fit or not. If yes, let's sign a deal. If not, how else can we help each other?

→ **Magical Board Presentation:** The entrepreneur brings their latest prototypes and visual updates of the company. The board comments, asks questions and maybe votes on these artifacts to provide more clarity and confidence to the entrepreneur as they continue forth.

→ **Magical Conference:** All participants have a clear understanding of all the options of how to spend their time at the conference. They get to network, contribute and be exposed to others who are passionate about the topic that brought them all there. As a facilitator or producer of this large event, you ensured there were

> breakouts/modules/interactive moments to empower each participant to contribute and try out their new knowledge or make a connection.

In all of these examples, the meeting facilitator helped everyone "Do the Work in the Meeting." It is one of our dearest magical meeting mantras. And by the end of this book, you will have the ability to understand the other mantras AND develop your own mantras to make your meetings more magical.

The rest of the non-obvious tips in the book are the advanced details of how to make each meeting (regardless of type) more magical, thus preventing your participants from regretting your request for their time and instead looking forward to your next calendar invite.

WHY YOU SHOULD READ THIS BOOK ...

Meetings are the underappreciated weapon that companies, teams and cultures use to be pioneers and leave their competition behind. The problem is that most of the time, meetings are misused.

You can prevent bad meetings from happening both as a facilitator and as a participant; this has enormous cost savings for your team and the teams they interact with.

The future of work is going to need more human facilitators as we automate more of the mundane parts of work. Even though we're using more AI, we still need people to facilitate the messy and complex creativity among humans.

PART ONE

Before Your Meetings

CHAPTER 1

A Preparation Guide for Magical Meetings

Imagine you are being prepped for surgery. Before you get put under by the anesthesiologist, you ask whether the surgeon and team are good to go. The anesthesiologist says, "I think so, but I am not really sure. They will likely just wing it."

Would you want your surgeon to put together the plan for your operation just 15 minutes before it started? Or maybe simply walk in and freestyle it? Hell no! Yet so many of our meetings are run this way.

> It might not seem so at first glance, but a facilitator of magical meetings is analogous to a world-class surgeon.

A surgeon first ensures that surgery is necessary. If it is, they ensure their team understands the purpose of the surgery, the chosen procedure and tools needed for the operation and the protocols and safety measures to make sure nobody is distracted, and ensure an efficient use of time with immense clarity in communication.

A magical facilitator must have the same mindset when preparing their meetings.

1.1 Wait, Do We Actually Need a Meeting?

If you do not have a clear purpose for your meeting, then you don't need one. The best surgeons generally don't perform surgery when it isn't necessary.

The cost of an ineffective meeting is not always obvious, but it compounds. If you have a one-hour meeting with eight executives, you aren't just consuming one hour of company time. If the meeting is a waste of time, you have squandered a collective total of eight hours. Not only that, the terrible meeting may have interrupted the participants' deep focus on something more valuable. They might need significant recovery time to get back into it. Last but not least, a terribly planned meeting can lead to unnecessary decision fatigue. So the first rule of magical meetings is to consider whether you even need a meeting in the first place.

We recommend creating your own simple set of meeting preparation questions and sharing it across your organization. Here is a short one that we use.

Try our simple **Should We Even Have a Meeting? Test**. Ask yourself the following questions:

Should We Even Have a Meeting? Test

Y N

☐ ☐ *Is there a clear purpose for gathering people to meet?*

☐ ☐ *Is there an artifact/prototype to review?*

☐ ☐ *Is there going to be an artifact/prototype that we create after workshopping in the meeting?*

☐ ☐ *Will decisions that alter the direction of the project be made?*

☐ ☐ *Is this essentially a status update in disguise?*

If you answer "yes" to question #5, then your meeting is better off as an email or a write-up in your company's project management software. If you answer "yes" to one or more of questions #1–4, then your meeting is likely worthy of an official team gathering and it's time to move forward with planning.

> One easy route to suck the magic out of a meeting is to have a meeting that is just a status update.

What Kind of Meeting Are You Planning?

(i)	Informative	Update people on a status or give them a presentation
🎬	Explorative	Consider options and review artifacts
🌱	Generative	Generate ideas and/or artifacts
○✓	Decisive	Make decisions on artifacts and options

Meetings can be informative, explorative, generative, or decisive. We have rarely seen a magical meeting be purely informative. There isn't anything wrong with informative meetings, but ideally this style is paired with another of the meeting functions. For example, your meeting's primary purpose could be to generate ideas and concepts (generative), but may have several informative moments throughout to help people generate more successfully.

Think this through ahead of time before expending any more resources. If there isn't a clear purpose and work to be done in the meeting, it may not be worth having at all.

Once you complete your Should We Even Have a Meeting? Test, you can share the answers with all attendees ahead of time and mention them at the start of your meeting.

Your attendees will better understand why this meeting is necessary, and hopefully they will look forward to contributing.

1.2	**Let's Cancel in Person but Meet Virtually**

Sometimes we can strategically cancel an in-person meeting and facilitate it online instead. Virtual meetings allow us to strategically accommodate many time zones and include participants who aren't able to travel. They also allow us to unbundle our workshops, spreading an eight-hour workshop across two to four days.

Ask yourself:

- What is your purpose and what outcome(s) do you seek?

- Who are the ideal participants? Does it make more sense to meet in person, or is it better for all desired participants to do a virtual workshop because it is less stressful for them and we can save money on travel?

- What is your meeting trying to accomplish, and can that best be achieved in person or online?

Those are the considerations of a magical meeting facilitator.

> Logistics-only thinking has resulted in less diverse gatherings because the facilitators didn't consider that they could convene more diverse minds online.

You would never fly someone from Shanghai to Austin to have a two-hour workshop on Monday and another on Friday. Even if that were the perfect design for the content and the arc of decision-making, it's just too expensive. Online, however, the logistics are different. Once you embrace virtual facilitation, you will realize there are some things you CAN'T do in person.

1.3   **Double Preparations When You Workshop Virtually**

If you are running a virtual workshop, you need to have twice the amount of preparation time and double your facilitator count. If you are the main facilitator, you need a co-facilitator to help you manage all of the online tools and read the virtual room.

Why is it important to double your prep time and to have a co-facilitator?

In a virtual meeting space, you need to invest extra time prepping the virtual environment so that each participant has a place to work alone, in addition to a place for group work. You also have to make sure people are able to find their workspace and haven't checked out.

Get started with some of our templates. ←

Having another facilitator participating is a smart contingency plan in case the internet connection drops or you have technical difficulties. Most importantly, it is nearly impossible to provide instructions and guidance to participants while also documenting key moments of the workshop. These roles can be split up between two facilitators.

Essential Virtual Workshop Prep Items

✓ **Create a workstation for each workshop participant**

For your workshop, make sure each participant has their digital equivalent of a desk. Ensure their solo workspace is labeled with their name, easy to find and annotated with self-explanatory instructions. Expect that they will not read your detailed instructions in an email.

✓ **Conduct a Virtual Workshop Orientation**

Do a brief virtual orientation before the meeting so the team understands the virtual workshop journey they are about to go on. We recommend making sure they know how to find their workspace, how to use the tools, what is expected of them, what is going to happen, and why they are even doing this.

✓ **Recruit a Co-Facilitator**

Identify, recruit and then brief your co-facilitator. Your co-facilitator can assist people in the exercises and take notes while you focus on keeping everyone on time, and answer questions as they arise. This can be helpful outside of workshops, too: If you are facilitating a sales meeting, one person can be listening and taking notes while the other is deeply engaged in the conversation.

1.4 Create Meeting Safety with Context and Rules

Online or offline, you need to communicate your meeting content and meeting rules ahead of time.

In a short, pre-meeting message to participants or in your calendar invite, include the following boilerplate to make the purpose and ground rules of the meeting clear:

→ **Meeting Purpose:** Share why this meeting is happening (use your Should We Have a Meeting? Test answers from Chapter 1.1). Get people excited: Explain why this meeting is important and what participants will contribute to and/or get out of it.

→ **Meeting Outline:** Give people an overview of the meeting. You don't need to go in depth into the schedule simply outline the boot-up time, major activities, break times, etc.

→ **Meeting Rules:** Let people know how you want them to behave (i.e., one speaker at a time, no leaving the meeting except for emergencies) and outline any other ground rules. For in-person meetings, one of our default ground rules is to put away smartphones.

Sometimes participants won't read this ahead of time and that is ok. You should also review all of these items at the start of your meeting to begin with context and rules that create a sense of safety.

1.5	**Invite Others Who Can See What You Can't**

Invite people outside of the core project team to workshop with you.

Once you have your meeting purpose set, consider the following question in your planning: Who has an opinion or perspective about this opportunity that we don't?

Rather than assume or brainstorm what a user or potential partner wants, invite them to the meeting to give the entire group an opportunity to connect and see things from others' perspectives. Some of your best meetings could be co-creating with customers, other companies, experts, communities and even internal teams that don't normally create together.

Mix it up by inviting new people. →

If you are going to invite outsiders, it is important to also prepare a win-win situation. Ask the potential participant what they are hoping to achieve or understand regarding your initiative and make sure that this is baked into your meeting narrative.

> Inviting outside participants can increase enthusiasm because new perspectives bring more energy.

Including outside opinions and thoughts can help make a compelling and meaningful meeting narrative. Don't limit your ideas.

1.6 Being a Meeting-Room Architect

The art of venue selection and space arrangements changes up the meeting dynamics. By changing the environment, you will change people's behavior.

If you want to have a straightforward deep dive on an important decision, try holding a walking meeting.

Looking to keep your prototype review short and sweet with only essential, constructive feedback? Make it a standing meeting with the prototype as the central point, or a copy of it handed out to each participant.

Leading a team to think about and sketch far-out, futuristic innovation ideas? Host your workshops at a different location each time to invite fresh modes of thinking and open-mindedness.

Have an immediate need for a workshop on a pressing issue? Spin up a virtual whiteboard and get your group together quickly to create a team improv vision board. Drop in pictures and other visual components to get them in the correct mindset.

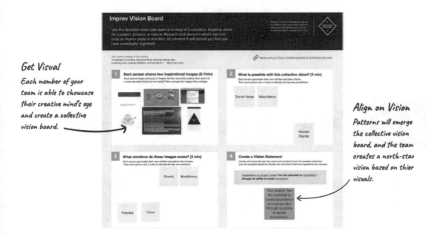

Get Visual
Each member of your team is able to showcase their creative mind's eye and create a collective vision board.

Align on Vision
Patterns will emerge the collective vision board, and the team creates a north-star vision based on thier visuals.

VISIT ONLINE RESOURCES FOR
Ideation exercises with our templates and guides at www.magicalmeetings.com.

Just as an architect thinks about the dance between form and function, you can do the same with your meeting environments.

1.7   Center the Purpose of Your Meeting with 9 Whys

If you are ever struggling with justifying a meeting's purpose, 9 Whys is a tried-and-true form of co-creation that helps you quickly reveal a compelling purpose and move forward with clarity on a meeting. In the worst case, you will decide you shouldn't have a meeting!

Ask up to nine "Why?" questions with stakeholders prior to your meeting so that when you kick it off, you remind people of why you are meeting and why the work matters. Here is an example...

> Do not try to establish your meeting's purpose on the fly.

If you are calling the meeting or are being asked to facilitate a meeting, this exercise is helpful to do beforehand; the answers to the deeper "Why?" questions can be a powerful way to start the meeting or workshop. This reminds the participants of why they are gathering and why they are needed to work on something meaningful.

Use 9 Whys To Find a Deeper Purpose

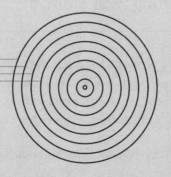

1. Why are we meeting to prototype a new product idea?
Example Answer: Because we need to innovate in the market.

2. Why is that important for us to do?
Example Answer: Because our customers' need and preferences are changing.

3. Why are their preferences changing?
Example Answer: Because with e-commerce and environmental sustainability, they have higher expectations for supply-chain transparency.

4. Why ... and so on

Ultimately, be sure you can answer the following five questions before you meet. If you are brought in to facilitate someone else's meeting, discuss these questions with them before planning the meeting. This will help you create an agenda tailored to the group you will be working with.

1. Why are we holding this workshop?

2. What do we want to have produced? How will we know we've been successful?

3. Who needs to be involved and what are their perspectives?

4. What concerns are likely to arise? What are the challenges that might get in our way?

5. What steps should we take during the meeting to achieve our purpose?

CHAPTER SUMMARY
KEY TAKEAWAYS:

- If you don't have a clear purpose for the meeting, do the right thing and cancel it; if you are a participant, make sure you understand the purpose before contributing.

- Change up your meeting environment and your participants; bring in fresh ideas by bringing new perspectives to your meeting.

- If your meeting ends up virtual, double your prep time and bring a co-facilitator.

CHAPTER 2

Why Most Meeting Agendas Suck

Nobody wants to attend a meeting that's boring, poorly planned, or stressful. And just because you have an agenda doesn't mean that it is any good.

> If your agenda is rigid, you will find it difficult to adapt to changes unfolding in the meeting.

An adaptive agenda will increase the odds of executing a successful and focused meeting that your attendees will feel good about. Adaptive means we are resilient to change. We make an agenda so we are prepared, and we must also be prepared to react to change during the meeting as needed.

Let's understand what makes your agendas go from rigid to adaptive.

2.1 **Start with the Why and What**

When you start planning a meeting, start with the why; without a clear purpose, there is no reason to hold a meeting. Make sure you can clearly articulate *why* you are having this meeting and *what* you need to accomplish by the end. If you can't identify the *why* and *what*, you won't be able to build a robust agenda.

Once you are clear on your *why* and have decided that it's a substantial reason to call a meeting, identify the objective of the meeting. Your objective may be to generate new ideas, explore potential solutions, seek input for a decision, receive help in making a decision, or something else entirely.

> Whatever it is, your objective will determine how you structure your agenda.

For example, if you wish to seek input for a decision, the meeting will likely include time for open discussion and generative activities designed to help uncover novel ideas. If you are looking to receive help with an important decision, the meeting might also include time for a vote to reach a consensus among the group.

Identify the critical points you need to hit in your meeting and the methods you'll need to use to address them.

2.2   Crowdsourcing Objectives: Co-creating a new agenda

If you are creating a new type of meeting or workshop, it is crucial that the objective of your meeting is in service of the meeting's attendees. When people feel that the information being discussed doesn't pertain to them or that they lack the skill set to actively contribute, it is likely they will feel that this new meeting is a waste of their time.

Before finalizing your new meeting agenda, talk to your participants—find out what's on their minds and what they'd like to work on rather than just religiously following the new agenda you created.

Meet with your participants ahead of time to get their feedback before finalizing your meeting activities. This could be a short, 30-minute virtual meeting.

Here is a checklist for your short agenda co-creation meeting:

New Agenda Co-Creation Checklist

✓ Share the purpose and objective of the meeting with the team

✓ Have each person take 3 minutes to write down what fears or concerns they have about the meeting

✓ Have each person take 3 minutes to write down what they hope to get out of the meeting

✓ Ask whether anyone has activity ideas they would like to do to help the team achieve the objective

Afterward, you will be inspired by the concerns and desires of your participants and move on to finalizing your agenda with all of that in mind. You might even find this "pre-meeting" with your future attendees will change your initial meeting activities entirely.

2.3 Get Ahead of It: Understanding the meeting before the meeting

An agenda serves as the roadmap for your meeting. It is a carefully designed plan that outlines the exact activities that will take place during your session, including the allotted time each activity or topic will last, as well as the start, end, and break times. It is your meeting's compass.

The most effective way to ensure that everyone is on the same page is to send them the agenda a few days beforehand. This allows everyone the opportunity to look it over, consider their contributions to what will be discussed and prepare any research or material that they may need beforehand.

Keep expectations low. ←

Sometimes you need your team to do pre-work before the meeting. For example, each person may need to curate a mood board for the project vision, or each participant may document their team's needs and share that at the meeting.

In any case, here is a solid checklist to follow:

Before The Meeting Checklist

✓ Include the agenda and how each person will contribute

✓ Explicitly say what you need from each person

✓ Also share this need separately with each meeting participant

✓ Send a reminder of your needs a day before the meeting

Don't make your team members scramble to find information or material that they want to reference on the spot; give them the opportunity to prepare artifacts before everyone is gathered.

It is also beneficial to prepare physical copies of the agenda to hand out or display on a project/whiteboard from the start of the meeting. A visual reference present throughout the session helps to keep the group on task. It also serves as a reminder for attendees for what is up next.

This mindset can also be applied to your virtual meetings.

Virtual Meeting Prep Tips

✓ Share a short screenshare video of you going over the agenda

✓ Having a short video as your main message will make your requests more human

✓ Provide a shared folder link for everyone to place their pre-work artifacts

✓ Post up the digital agenda onto your digital workroom and your team communication systems

VISIT ONLINE RESOURCES FOR
Free meeting preparation resources at magicalmeetings.com.

2.4   Timing a Meeting: When to meet and for how long

A study conducted by UK-based scheduling firm You Can Book Me found that the optimal time to book a meeting is Tuesday at 2:30 p.m. (based on data from two million responses to 530,000 meeting invitations). Tuesday meetings avoid the Monday Blues without being too late in the week, which means people are still refreshed from the weekend but have gotten back into the swing of the work week. The 2:30 p.m. time frame allows employees the morning to get into work mode (i.e., be in a place of optimal focus and collaboration) without being so late that their mind is on post-work responsibilities such as housework or childcare.

> While it's unrealistic to schedule every meeting on Tuesday at 2:30 p.m., holding meetings mid-afternoon and midweek is a general guideline you can follow.

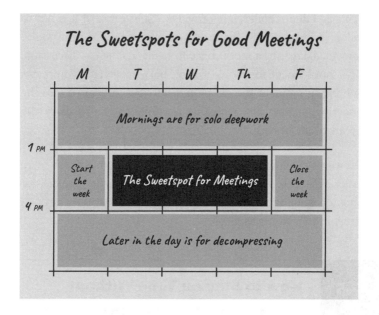

The length of your meeting is also significant: Too long of a meeting causes a decrease in attention span, retention, and attendees' ability to make good decisions, while having a moderate level of pressure—such as a time restraint—can lead to optimal performance.

We are fans of a 45-minute meeting for most meeting types. We also see our workshops as a collection of these 45-minute sessions.

The 45-minute meeting is 10 minutes of boot-up time, a 30-minute activity that includes all participants, and five minutes to finalize next steps and ownership.

This 45-minute boilerplate provides a light sense of urgency to address and flesh out the meeting's purpose in the time you've provided, creating a more concentrated and efficient discussion. It is short enough for people to avoid burnout, and it incorporates a boot-up moment to help participants get integrated into the meeting. It also has a closing portion that helps carry the momentum forward.

Start playfully before you get to work.

However much time you decide to allot for your meeting, be sure to end on time. Finishing on time is respecting the time of your attendees and sets a precedent for professionalism, efficiency, and trust in your future agendas.

2.5   How to Stay on Time Without Being a Timeline Dictator

Assign specific time frames to each activity and don't be afraid to stick to them. Many facilitators are hesitant to closely follow time frames in a meeting for fear of seeming authoritarian, but this can be a mistake. Remember that light sense of urgency we've created by applying a time restraint? It will disappear if attendees do not sense that the agenda will be followed closely.

Do not, however, become inflexible. You may find that specific topics need more time than you've allotted once you're in the meeting. If this happens, adjust wisely to accommodate for the need while also ensuring you do not run the meeting longer than scheduled.

Pro tip: Use a dynamic agenda tool such as SessionLab or a Google Sheet so you can recalculate timing when you adjust your meeting on the fly.

> If a meaningful conversation happens and takes up more time than expected, acknowledge that you're going over the time allotted for the exercise and figure out where to shave off time later in the agenda. If necessary, check in with the team to get their feedback on how to pivot.

It is common to underestimate the time required to address a topic and all that comes with it: answering questions, reaching a group understanding of varying points of view, creating possible solutions and coming to a consensus after a thoughtful discussion. Do the math and determine the appropriate amount of time necessary to address each topic adequately. Time frames also help keep attendees on task. When there is a limited amount of time for an activity, they must use it wisely; this means sticking to the topic, not oversharing, and making their responses concise.

To reduce the risk of running out of time, pad each activity on your agenda by 20%. If you are new to an activity, or you are planning a big decision-making moment, double the amount of time.

> If you feel that you can discuss something and come to a consensus in 10 minutes, plan for 20 minutes.

We also recommend scaling back your expectations of what you'll accomplish in your meeting. You need more time than you might think for each individual activity. Keep your objective in mind and eliminate anything on your agenda that isn't in service of that objective. If you are doing a generic warmup or icebreaker, figure out how to make it align with your purpose.

And just in case your meeting suddenly veers off course, because sometimes participants get off-topic or unfocused, these are two questions you should start getting comfortable asking:

Is this getting us closer to or farther from our goal?

That's a good point. For now, can we put that on the issues list so we don't forget it and get back to ____?

2.6 The Magical Beauty of Intentional Breaks

If you are planning a more extended meeting, be sure to build in ample time for breaks. You probably need one or two more than you think.

If you are running a virtual meeting, remind your participants about screen fatigue. Encourage them to turn off their cameras and go for a quick walk during breaks. Step away and rebuild your own enthusiasm.

> We recommend setting a break every 60–90 minutes if your meeting is multiple hours.

People need decompression time and, of course, time to check their email or Slack messages in case there is a pressing issue.

By allowing your attendees time to relax and take care of matters unrelated to your meeting, you're limiting the amount of time that their minds wander during the meeting itself. You're also allowing them to hit their reset buttons and return clearheaded and focused. Employees who feel refreshed will generate better ideas and more thoughtful discussion.

Keep the snacks healthy for energy! →

Additionally, if your budget allows it, definitely bring in snacks, coffee, water, etc. to keep people from getting "hangry" and distracted.

Rest is essential. Your participants thank you in advance for respecting that.

2.7	**Five Ways to Create More "Flow" in Your Next Meeting**

A good meeting stays on task, ends on time, and reaches its objective by the end; a great meeting creates a sense of flow: the positive mental state of being completely absorbed by, focused on and involved in your activities at a certain point in time, as well as deriving enjoyment from being engaged in that activity.

Here are some tips to help you go beyond your agenda and create a sense of flow for your participants.

TIP 1 ELIMINATE UNNECESSARY TOPICS

Be sure to eliminate any topics or talking points that do not serve the purpose of the meeting or help you achieve your objective. Any time spent discussing irrelevant content is precious time taken away from achieving the goal, including unpurposeful team building exercises!

TIP 2 DEVELOP A PROGRESSION

Clearly define the essential topics that need to be addressed and stick to them. Each topic should serve as a segment of the meeting. Outline them in order of importance or relevance to create a natural flow as the meeting unfolds. Your meeting should feel like it is building upon itself; each step in the agenda should be crucial to tackling the next. This fosters a sense of progress and accomplishment that keeps attendees not only engaged but proud of the work they are doing.

TIP 3 CONSIDER YOUR NARRATIVE ARC

Consider the narrative arc of your meeting. You will gain the most valuable insight from your team members if you consider the order in which relevant information or activities will be shared with them. After entering the room, begin by providing attendees with the context that they may need to consider when tackling the meeting material.

TIP 4 ESTABLISH A SHARED STARTING POINT

Ask questions to ensure that everyone understands where the group is starting from. Make sure to support those who are a few steps behind and adjust your start point. You may even need to adjust your agenda to support this new starting point. Only then is it safe to dive into discussions and activities in search of your objective.

TIP 5 FOCUS ON CREATING FLOW

Order the discussions and activities such that they will build on each other. When later work relies on earlier work, you are constrained in a pleasant and productive way. Be sure to end by debriefing and reflecting on the insights gained during every step in your agenda so that it is clear how later activities will be impacted.

Always structure your meeting to flow linearly, step by step, from purpose to objective.

2.8 The Art of Debriefing: Focus on the Last Five Minutes

It is imperative to schedule time to debrief before the end of a meeting. Taking time to summarize and reflect on what was discussed, the information that was shared, and the decision that was reached ensures everyone knows what to expect moving forward. It also synthesizes the material touched upon to ensure that everyone walks away with the same understanding of where the meeting ended and how that point was reached.

Be sure you and all attendees can answer these questions:

→ What decisions were made?

→ What are your next steps? How can you apply what was learned in an impactful way?

→ What needs to be done when, and by whom, to bring the idea to life?

We recommend having these questions already drafted on your physical or digital whiteboard so that they are top of mind throughout the meeting.

Ask for 2 days. 2 weeks. and 2 months commitments.

Debriefing should include commitments from participants. Have people commit to specific tasks or duties to perform after the meeting. The postmeeting work will build upon the momentum created in the meeting and start to bring meeting objectives to life.

Before you end the meeting, express gratitude and appreciation for your attendees. When people feel appreciated and as though they are a meaningful part of a group, they are more inclined to give their best day in and day out. Tell your team what they've done or are doing well, with no catch other than to genuinely thank them. Show them some love, and it will return tenfold.

We are usually able to facilitate both commitment and appreciation in about 10–15 minutes.

2.9 Rethink Your Old Habits and Lazy Rituals

Backward design (starting with the end goal and backtracking your strategies from there) is crucial not only to building your agenda, but also for designing the activities that will fill it. Just as you must let your objective lead the way when planning a meeting, so too must your desired outcome guide your methods. Don't get stuck in old habits or rituals that do not properly serve your goal. Consider ditching frameworks created by others and developing a method specifically designed to deliver your desired outcome.

Trying to shoehorn in a system built for other teams or other projects will only end in both you and your team feeling frustrated and stalled. Clear your mind of method bias and reverse engineer your meeting activities to reach the outcome you want.

Don't settle for an answer that's too vague or broad when determining your desired outcome; drill down to the core of what you're looking for. What are the deliverables you seek? What are you building? What does *done* look like? The better you understand what it is you're looking to create, the more targeted you can be when devising your plan of attack.

This isn't to say that you must construct every activity from scratch. Some methods are truly versatile.

However, if you find yourself using the same few methods in every meeting, take it as a sign that you need to check whether or not your methods are in service of your outcome.

We worked with a group of designers and facilitators who had only been using Design Sprint exercises for their workshops, month after month. After attending one of our trainings, they became curious about an additional facilitation framework called Liberating Structures.[2] We heard back from them a few weeks later, and they couldn't stop talking about how the new microactivity structures were unleashing meeting participants who weren't previously engaging. Sure, they will still use Design Sprints, but they now have an expanded toolkit of methods that they can more accurately pair with certain workshop objectives. Expanding your toolkit isn't only going to help you; it has the potential to empower all of your participants as well.

If you are looking to experiment with new facilitation methods, we have plenty of meeting activity templates and a weekly online meetup where you can practice them. Go to www.magicalmeetings.com to get started.

2.10 Why Deadlines Are So Important— and How to Use Them

Analysis paralysis is deadly to productivity; when examining gives way to *overexamining* and thinking turns into *overthinking*, we never quite hit the *doing* part of the creation process. It may be tempting to throw increasingly more time and money at a problem or process in order to avoid making a wrong decision, but this is a mistake. Always set deadlines. More often than not, decisions are reversible; it is better to find out you've made the wrong decision and then make the right one than to spend infinity going back and forth about how to move forward.

Deadlines keep your team moving forward for the same reason limiting how long your meeting runs does—that light sense of urgency. When we create constraints by intentionally limiting our time, we're more focused.

Using deadlines in your meetings:

→ Set deadlines both within and outside your meeting.

→ When planning activities, be clear about how long attendees have for the activity and what they need to accomplish by the end of that time. Make it visual with a timer.

→ Rather than waiting for everyone to complete a task, give them a warning that it will be time to move on soon. First ask, "Who needs one more minute?" Then declare, "Thirty more seconds; time to wrap up."

→ When assigning duties for team members to complete after the meeting is over, be clear about when those duties need to be completed.

Postmeeting deadlines will keep meeting material on the minds of attendees after they leave the physical space. This will prevent all of the work done in the meeting from evaporating as soon as the meeting is over.

CHAPTER SUMMARY
KEY TAKEAWAYS:

- You shouldn't be the only one creating the agenda, and it needs to be designed with purpose.

- Your agenda should account for next steps and accountability.

- Intentionally set breaks during the meeting or workshops; breaks keep the flow going, and we all deserve them.

CHAPTER 3

How to Pick the Right Structure for Your Meeting

Rather than being composed of an hour-long PowerPoint presentation or endless debate, your meetings need structure, purposeful activities, and philosophies that facilitate collaborative work among attendees.

There is a vast library of preexisting frameworks and methods available to you to help you build a meeting that will get your team to their objective in a way that liberates them to participate and care.

In the next few chapters, we will introduce some of our favorites based on common meeting needs.

3.1	**The Right Meeting Structure for Generating Ideas**

These methods can be applied to gatherings of any size and work best for meetings that will mostly be focused on exploring new concepts.

The goal is to empower each participant to contribute in meaningful ways that move you toward the objective rather than sitting back and letting the facilitator do all of the heavy lifting.

SCAMPER is a method of focused brainstorming. Rather than just saying "Come up with ideas!", SCAMPER runs you through seven techniques for idea generation: Substitute, Combine, Adapt, Modify, Put to another use, Eliminate and Reverse.

Crazy 8s is an activity that we run as part of every Design Sprint, but it can be used anytime you want each participant to come up with a bunch of visual ideas quickly. It is an excellent rapid form of prototyping.

10 x 10 Writing is a really cool writing exercise when you need to just get people thinking in silence instead of talking over each other.

How to Remix Anything is a canvas you can use when you want to use analogous inspiration to reveal truly novel solutions.

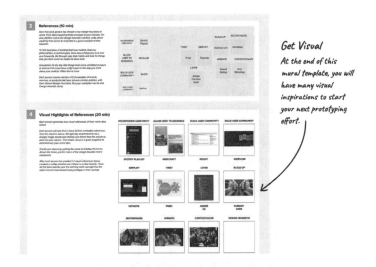

Get Visual

At the end of this mural template, you will have many visual inspirations to start your next prototyping effort.

VISIT ONLINE RESOURCES FOR

These ideation exercises with our templates and guides at www.magicalmeetings.com.

3.2 | # The Right Meeting Structure for Creating Alignment

Misalignment is inevitable. We can all be gathered in a room with the same positive intentions, yet we haven't taken the time to synchronize our context and understand the purpose. We use these exercises to align on what we are doing and what we are not doing. We recommend using these structured exercises earlier in your meeting.

9-Word Purpose is a really quick Mad Lib–style activity to get people a rough draft for a mission statement, and is really handy for a team charter.

Hopes & Fears provides a quick assessment of what expectations and concerns the participants are bringing into the room.

Triz helps you spot counterproductive behavior that is slowing you down. You will bring it to the surface and blow it up so you can stop being your own worst enemy.

Focus Finder is a four-part reflection process to help you find a refreshing focus on any initiative at any moment of its timeline.

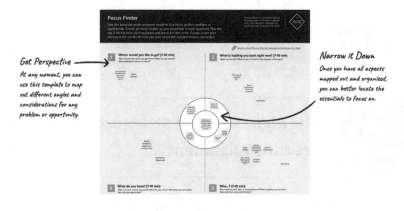

Get Perspective —
At any moment, you can use this template to map out different angles and considerations for any problem or opportunity.

Narrow it Down
Once you have all aspects mapped out and organized, you can better locate the essentials to focus on.

VISIT ONLINE RESOURCES TO
Start aligning your team with our templates and guides at www.magicalmeetings.com.

3.3 The Right Meeting Structure for Strategizing and Making Things Happen

Ok, you generated a bunch of ideas, stickies, or sketches. What is next and how do you move forward? These are great activities to run after your creative ideation structures or modules.

What, So What, Now What is a great tool for going from reflection to action in a systematic way.

Note & Vote is a method that comes from the book *Sprint*[3] by Jake Knapp, John Zeratsky, and Braden Kowitz. It gives everyone an equal vote when making a decision. It's super simple but highly effective. We use it in any meeting, any day of the week.

Affinity Grouping helps you identify big themes in a large group of ideas. We use this method to synthesize sticky-note storms and other brainstorming activities. Take the ideas generated by the group and begin to cluster like ideas together.

Start Within Canvas is excellent when you want to bust assumptions and truly unleash creative change inside of your company.

Critical Uncertainties helps the entire team develop alternate strategies for different future potential outcomes.

Team Strength Library lets you take stock of your team's unique array of strengths and examine how you can apply them to your current objectives to optimize each person's personality.

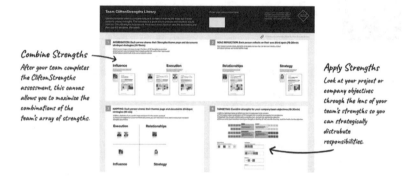

Combine Strengths

After your team completes the CliftonStrengths assessment, this canvas allows you to maximize the combinations of the team's array of strengths.

Apply Strengths

Look at your project or company objectives through the lens of your team's strengths so you can strategically distribute responsibilities.

VISIT ONLINE RESOURCES TO
Map your ideas to execution with our templates and guides at www.magicalmeetings.com.

3.4 The Right Meeting Structure for More Connection with Your Participants

---

Use these structured exercises toward the opening of your meeting. Participants will quickly gain new perspectives on the people they'll be working with throughout the meeting or day, and start with a spark of connection and playfulness.

Impromptu Networking is a great way to start off your gathering with some human connection that is still on topic. It's also handy for virtual meetings when you need a soft start to account for tardy participants. By the end, each person will talk to around four people and learn something new about their colleagues or teammates.

Team Bookshelf is a fun exercise that honors each person's passion and interests with the vehicle of their favorite book.

Team Improv Vision Board helps the team align on a visual mood board and then draft a peer-to-peer mission statement.

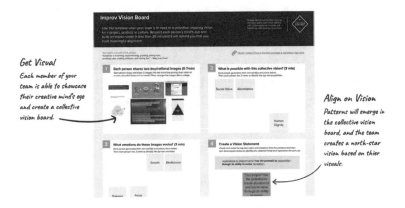

Get Visual
Each member of your team is able to showcase their creative mind's eye and create a collective vision board.

Align on Vision
Patterns will emerge in the collective vision board, and the team creates a north-star vision based on thier visuals.

VISIT ONLINE RESOURCES TO
Start using these team-bonding activities with our templates and guides at www.magicalmeetings.com.

3.5 Buffer Time: How to Prevent Stragglers

The first step to keeping a meeting—virtual or in-person—running on time is to start on time. Starting meetings on time will send a strong signal that it is important to show up on time. Remember Blockbuster's infamous late fees? You could institute a late fee of your own. Collect the proceeds to fund innovative meeting technology.

With so many varying schedules and wandering headspaces, not everyone shows up to a meeting in the same place. For example, some people may be rushing from one session to the next, unable to quiet the busy chatter in their heads and experiencing brain fog because of it; others might be trying to break out of a midday funk.

> Setting aside even five minutes at the beginning of the meeting to center everyone in the same headspace can drastically improve collaboration, attention and performance.

Don't Always End on The Hour

One reason most people are late to meetings is that there was no buffer time between meetings. Ever dealt with this kind of calendar with no buffer time?

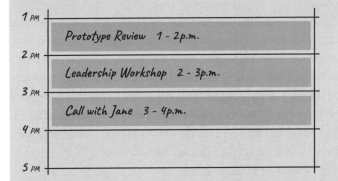

Ending before the end of an hour is a more manageable exsperience for these same meetings:

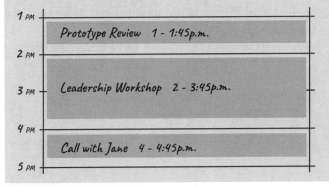

Ever started a meeting with a few minutes of breathing or listening to a peaceful song? Practicing mindfulness through group meditation is one option. Once attendees have found their seats, you can play a short guided meditation for the group. Five minutes' meditation is all that's necessary to experience a decrease in stress levels and an increase in presence, focus and performance.

If your organization is large and/or holding multiple meetings that some people may be attending back-to-back, we recommend using Google Calendar's Speedy Meeting function. When scheduling a meeting via Google Calendar, check the "Speedy Meeting" box to end a 30-minute meeting five minutes early or a 60-minute meeting 10 minutes early. You can also make this your calendar's default by going into your settings. This allows a buffer for meeting attendees to get their computer, tools and resources set up for their next meeting without being late.

Attendees who know they have buffer time to make it to their next meeting are less likely to mentally check out toward the end of your meeting due to stress or anxiety about rushing to their next meeting.

Virtual = More Buffer

In general, we believe that the pace of online meetings needs to be slower than that of in-person meetings. While technology can indeed speed us up, it can also slow us down. That's because virtual gatherings must account for many factors that don't exist when we're connecting face-to-face.

For example, there is a limited ability to read the virtual room intelligence to ensure that everyone is on the same page. The physical separation and low bandwidth signals make it difficult to notice when someone is distracted, struggling, or falling behind. If you do manage to detect that someone needs help, it takes extra time to stop and catch them up.

Simply put, things take longer online. There are inevitably delays and extra processing time needed to get everyone on board. Account for extra buffer time to set up and field mishaps during your meeting. You'll also need to prepare to support those who are less familiar with the tools you've chosen or having trouble with their internet connection.

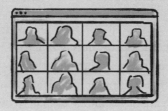

| 3.6 | **How to Effectively Use Time Constraints for Better Ideas** |

Constraints breed innovation. When given too much time to think, people are prone to *overthinking* and allowing their inner critic to censor their best ideas. Setting a time constraint for your team is crucial for eliminating analysis paralysis and encouraging ideas that come from outside the box. It also instills a light pressure that prevents team members from getting distracted by happenings outside of the room. When time is of the essence, being present in the moment comes much more naturally.

Unfortunately, people aren't particularly fond of timers. Bringing out a kitchen timer or putting up a countdown can often cloud peoples' thoughts with anxiety. Not all hope is lost, however. Here's how you can use a timer in a meeting without stirring dread in your attendees.

TIP 1 DON'T GLOSS OVER THE INTRODUCTION OF YOUR TIMER

Use this moment as an opportunity to frame the timer as a helpful tool rather than an oppressive force lurking in the background. Remind your team that the timer is their key to achieving the goal on time. They do not have unlimited time, so of course they will not be able to perfect all of their ideas before sharing. Sharing imperfect ideas encourages co-creation by raising potential issues faster and allowing team members to build on each other's ideas. The timer gives them the freedom to think in pieces rather than in perfection, which in turn gives way to more novel solutions.

TIP 2 USE A TIMER WITH A WARNING

Let the room know before the activity starts that you will be giving time warnings. Team members will be able to relax and be present knowing that they will be notified when they should begin wrapping up. A simple, large physical timer such as the Time Timer, of Design Sprint fame, is great because participants can intuitively understand the proportion of time remaining.

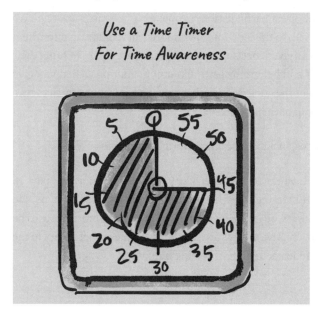

TIP 3 HAVE GOOD TIMER TASTES

Put some thought into the aesthetics of the timer that you choose. Giant red digital numbers that count down and end in aggressive beeping may set a much more ominous mood than you're hoping for; consider using something more neutral, relaxing, or even funny instead. There are countless physical and virtual timers available to you—find something that feels right for the mood you want to set.

3.7 Make Your Meetings Optional

To enable great participation, we make our meetings optional. We think it's up to the individual to choose whether it's right for them to attend a given meeting; you want each participant to bring their best self and be enthusiastic about contributing. When you give employees the choice of whether to attend, you allow them to take ownership of their time.

In essence, making meetings optional eliminates excuses.

Make sure
to let people
know you are
going to miss.

If people value doing other work over being an active part in a certain meeting, they have the freedom to do so. The people who *choose* to be in the meeting, then, are much more likely to be engaged, creative and responsive. This elevates productivity in the room and leads to better meeting outcomes.

Finally, when you embrace making meetings optional, you can learn from all the meeting declines. Ask your participants to send you a short description of why they are declining the meeting. Their reasoning for not coming will help you refine your ongoing approach to inviting participants.

CHAPTER SUMMARY
KEY TAKEAWAYS:

- Experiment with new meeting frameworks and activities to build excitement and unleash more participation for your upcoming meetings.

- Be generous with buffer time.

- Confidently use a timer; it not only keeps us on track, but helps stir up ideation.

- Making meetings optional can help you ensure that the meeting enthusiasm is high.

PART TWO

During Your Meetings

CHAPTER 4

How to Do the Work in the Meeting (Not After)

How much more willing would you be to attend a meeting if you knew it wasn't all talk? When you start focusing on doing work in the meeting rather than afterward, your meetings aren't so dull. They turn into working sessions instead of slogs. There are concrete things to talk about. You can repair and correct things in real time, resulting in less to fix later. Everyone's excited and engaged, so more gets done.

4.1 Prototypes, Not Action Items: Weathering the Sticky-Note Storm

You've likely fallen victim to the "Sticky Storm," a half-baked workshop that involves a tornado of sticky notes but doesn't result in any action. Ideas are flowing and there is lots of excitement, but afterward, the group reverts to business as usual. These tips can help you turn the chaos of a Sticky Storm into productive and structured workshops with real outcomes.

A "Sticky Storm" is a bunch of ideas on sticky notes without a clear action plan.

TIP 1 USE PROTOTYPES

If there isn't a clear, tangible prototype or solution concept to flesh out and explore, there is no reason to have a meeting in the first place. Nowadays, a prototype can take various forms. For a strategist or project manager, a prototype might consist of a storyboard, written brief, or sample pitch deck. A salesperson may have a product demo or webpage they are showcasing to a potential customer. A designer may make a mood board; a developer might quickly share a code snippet.

> Create whatever prototype best fits your needs, then plan your meeting to review and tweak it with your team.

A hunk of wood can be a prototype.

The takeaway is this: Prototypes don't have to be complicated. Test whether your new two-pound product is too heavy by asking potential users to carry around a two-pound weight for a couple of hours. Want to know whether 3 x 5 inches is a reasonable size for your new smartphone? Cut out a 3-x-5-inch piece of wood and carry it around in your pocket to see how it feels. The important thing is to focus on the question you are trying to answer or the abstract concept you need to make more tangible. Have participants bring prototypes to your meeting so you don't get lost in words and instead focus your attention on artifacts that allow you to visualize and interact with potential solutions for your objective.

TIP 2 VOTE AND DECIDE ON PROTOTYPES

Once you analyze and work on your prototypes, you need to narrow down options and determine which one to pursue. A standard decision technique is basic voting to find the consensus (more on that later in this chapter).

TIP 3 **ASSIGN COMMITMENT BUDDIES**

The most successful meetings end with a debrief of what was discussed and decided, and an understanding of how to proceed. This often includes having participants commit to tangible tasks to be completed by a set due date to keep the process moving forward. Have each participant choose a "commitment buddy" to hold them accountable for their commitments. Doing so will ensure everyone stays on track and contributes to the team innovation effort.

4.2	**Balancing Personalities: Group think and working alone together**

The social dynamics of group discussions can kill the momentum of a team's progress and drain it of its creative energy. Often the best ideas don't make the final cut. Usually the ones that do survive come from, or are endorsed by, the loudest or highest-ranking person in the room. Create space for everyone to contribute so you can extract wisdom from all participants, regardless of personality.

Introverts and extroverts alike will appreciate the power of working together, alone. We created the "Take-5 Method" for this.

THE TAKE-5 METHOD:

→ The facilitator sets the context of the problem or opportunity the team faces and instructs them to work silently instead of engaging in group discussion.

→ Each person spends five minutes working on the same task in silence, jotting down thoughts and sketching thumbnails of their vision.

→ Each person then shares their prototype with the team.

→ The facilitator then leads a debrief to help all participants understand trends and outliers, as well as decide on next steps.

This method allows each person time to visually capture detail in their ideas. Showing the idea instead of only talking about it results in more clarity and less risk of someone being misunderstood. Your less outgoing team members will also have the opportunity to fully prepare their idea before presenting to the group rather than having to juggle public speaking and idea formation at the same time.

Take-5 is a great starting point to help your team do meaningful work in the meeting. Each artifact that participants create can be leveraged later by storing them in your meetings archive (more on this in Chapter 8).

Just as your team can benefit from working alone, together, so too can they benefit from working together, alone. Virtual teams can utilize a variety of programs and services to make communication and virtual collaboration efficient and effective. Just because your team is physically apart does not mean it cannot work together just as effectively as it would if participants were in the same space. These virtual tools will also level the playing field for team members who are less social or outspoken; they can let their work speak for itself.

VISIT ONLINE RESOURCES
If you're looking for meeting activities to help your team work together, alone, during virtual meetings, we recommend our app Control Room.

4.3	**Participatory Decision-Making**

Participatory decision-making is a decision-making style that calls for an entire group rather than an individual or a smaller subsection of the group to make all decisions. The idea is that this will lead to options that everyone in the group can support. It requires the group's leader to relinquish some amount of control, but provides team members with a sense of responsibility and inclusion that makes them more valuable contributors to the team in the long run.

> It is important to make sure that everyone agrees to support the decision, not that everyone agrees 100%.

Here are two decision-making frameworks you can use in your upcoming meetings.

1 MAKE A DECISION USING MAJORITY VOTES

This classic voting framework can be used in situations where the group is unable to please everyone, or the decision being made is trivial and not worth the amount of time it would take to come to a true consensus (for example, where to eat lunch or what color of an office supply to purchase). The majority vote is quick and a useful lifeline when a consensus is just not possible, but it does run the risk of alienating the group members who do not agree with the majority.

2 HAVE A "DECIDER" MAKE FINAL DECISIONS

If your group is making decisions that classify as an emergency or if participants are being asked to choose between two evils, it may be best to appoint a Decider who ultimately makes the final decision. Activities such as silent voting are conducted, allowing the Decider to see which idea the group is leaning toward. The decider considers this insight and makes a final call on which idea to pursue.

Having a preselected Decider in the meeting will guarantee an agreed-upon path forward. All participants in the meeting become advisors to the Decider so they can lean on them before making a final decision.

The Decider role comes from the book *Sprint* and is a critical element to the Design Sprint's usefulness as a tool to quickly solve tough problems. Considering that most decisions are reversible, the Design Sprint utilizes a Decider to make quick decisions that we can learn from and adjust course if needed.

Who should be the Decider? Depending on your situation, it should be the person who has the most influence, responsibility, or experience. The Decider must make a decision and explain their reasoning to all participants. This helps teams understand the consensus and the overall plan but does not require them to reach a point where everyone—or even almost everyone, agrees.

How to pick a good Decider:

1. They are decisive (duh!)

2. They are transparent and speak clearly

3. They possess authority

4. They are known for getting things done

5. They are great listeners

Many of the templates and activities we mentioned in Chapter 3 can be utilized to facilitate participatory decision-making. These activities may end in a consensus, giving the Decider the information they need to make an informed decision.

4.4   Room Intelligence: Nobody is as smart as Everybody

Talent wins games, but teamwork and intelligence wins championships.

–Michael Jordan

When it comes to exploring and creating new ideas, collaboration is much mightier than the brainpower of any one individual.

> We have meetings because of room intelligence; the collective intellect of an entire room is cleverer and more innovative than any one thinker.

Collective intelligence leads to more creativity, which produces more (and often better quality!) potential ideas and solutions. As a result, companies have better meetings and greater overall success.

An important aspect of extracting room intelligence is nurturing overall creativity in each individual team member as well as the group as a whole. A conscious, active effort to do so is crucial.

Bringing minds together in an environment that is both productive and focused requires a facilitator. This person has the seasoned ability to guide the group through discussion and structured activities. They can keep everyone on track, create a safe and creative environment for all, and ultimately ensure the group arrives at a decision by the end of the meeting.

Use the words "room intelligence" often. It helps remind everyone that we are in this together.

4.5	**Capture Room Intelligence**

To be able to say you did good work in a meeting, you need to capture the work that was done and organize it. Good meetings are constantly producing room intelligence, and it is the facilitator's responsibility to capture it. Don't wait until the end of the meeting to do so.

Make capturing a continuous activity in your meetings or as Josh Porter loves to say, "Always Be Capturing." If the activity is not self-documenting, design time into your agenda to account for transcribing. Remember: If you don't write it down, it didn't happen.

It's the facilitator's job to make sure room intelligence is captured.

To excel at continuous capturing, we recommend:

Create a place to store pictures and documentation of the work done in the meeting.

Plan capturing and storage time into your agenda. We recommend scheduling five minutes to capture and document at the end of each meeting activity.

An awesome way to have a multi-threaded meeting! ←

You don't have to do all the capturing alone. After each exercise, have participants help you document, organize and store what was captured. If everyone in the meeting is capturing, the work becomes multi-threaded. If three people write down reactions to something someone says, they will capture three different interpretations, diversifying your ideas.

If you do this proactively, you don't have to stay around after the meeting capturing and documenting everything.

Another skill facilitators bring to the table is their ability to cut through the noise, conversation, and debate and "bubble up" what the group is saying. They distill conversations and key discussion points and can summarize the group's thoughts.

One of our favorite techniques is to ask, "How should I capture that?" or even hand over the whiteboard marker and let them write it themselves.

Another great way to practice this in a meeting with a lot of dialog or debate is to silently capture what you are hearing. When you see a good opportunity, ask your participants, "Can I share with you all what I am hearing?" Walk them through the room intelligence you've captured. Ask them, "Did I get this right? How can I fix this?" If there are any points of disagreement or nuance, it's important to call attention to them so that you can repair issues before moving forward.

Finally, if you are doing your meeting exercises virtually on a digital whiteboard, you will have less work to do because you are essentially capturing in real time!

4.6   Competing Creativity

> *The strength of the team is each individual member. The strength of each member is the team.*
>
> – Phil Jackson

Creativity is arguably the most valuable asset your participants will bring to the table; it is what gives humans an edge over technology.

It makes each individual a valuable voice in the room, as it leads each of us to different ideas and innovations. On the flip side, friction can occur when two individuals face creative differences. Facilitators with the necessary skills to help unify individuals of all backgrounds are needed to encourage each team member's best work and ensure their voices are heard.

Psychological safety is one of the most important requirements for having a magical meeting. Attendees need to feel comfortable sharing their ideas and expressing their views. Inspire fluid and respectful communication by including everyone. This requires the facilitator to read the group, both verbally and nonverbally, and adjust to its needs throughout the meeting while keeping everyone focused. It is also beneficial to paraphrase the group progress that is being made as you go, and to reflect back all conclusions reached.

Diversity only matters if everyone is sharing.

Trust and empathy are essential components of building healthy and successful relationships within a group. Great facilitators possess the ability to identify and focus on the shared values, common goals, and mutual interests. Even when the room appears to be in alignment, don't assume you understand how all participants are feeling.

Check in with your participants frequently by asking each person how they are feeling.

Creating a safe container is essential to make the most of your meeting dynamics.

When conflict arises, it is important to immediately identify the cause or source to fully understand it before evaluating and discussing possible solutions. To healthily manage conflict, you must empathize with other people's viewpoints calmly and respectfully.

When Conflict Arises

✓ Quickly determine whether the conflict is based on content disagreements, misaligned values or external factors.

✓ Face conflict head-on to increase your chances of finding common ground.

✓ When participants are disagreeing, use phrases such as: "What is your understanding of what ____ is saying?" or "What evidence and reasons are there for ____ ?"

✓ Encourage the group to consider shared values and common goals rather than highlighting disagreements and ensure each team member has a clearly defined role, clarifying the distribution of responsibilities.

✓ Foster a sense of positivity and appreciation for what works.

✓ Defuse tensions by injecting a dose of humor to redirect the group's energy, initiate a well-timed break, or calm the room.

CHAPTER SUMMARY
KEY TAKEAWAYS:

- Work alone, together.

- Utilize prototypes to do meaningful work during, not after, the meeting.

- Practice participatory decision-making for more durable decisions.

- Always be capturing so you can leverage the room intelligence that occurred in the meeting.

- Embrace conflict as an opportunity to discover better ideas and clarity.

CHAPTER 5

How to Facilitate a Magical Meeting

Here is a bold mantra that will force you into adopting extreme ownership as a facilitator:

> There are no such things as bad meetings, just bad facilitators.

Don't take it personally. We mean it in the best way.

This chapter will take inspiration from the sci-fi epic *Star Wars*. For you to be a good facilitator, you must turn from the dark side of meeting facilitation and instead use the light side of the force. You must practice being graceful any time a meeting starts to get sabotaged.

Our friend and fellow Non-Obvious Guide author Sunni Brown once gave a talk at Control the Room, our facilitator summit. We wish you could have been there. She explained the difference between facilitators who are "strong with force" versus those who are "drunk with power." Facilitators with force possess and practice

May the force be with you. ←

curiosity, deep listening, responsiveness rather than reaction, and self-responsibility, and they are firm but not aggressive. Essentially, these are facilitators who embody the philosophy of the Jedi.

Conversely, facilitators obsessed with power are reactive rather than responsive, dominate the room, and lash out when their power is tested. They are filled with a dark side that prevents meetings from being magical for all participants. And if the participants don't find the meeting magical, it is the facilitator's fault.

Sunni is spot on. With the right mindset, you can be like Yoda in your meetings—a facilitator Jedi who can create magic in any meeting, regardless of what happens and who is in the room.

5.1 How to Handle Difficult Meeting Participants with Grace

He who takes offense when offense was not intended is a fool, yet he who takes offense when offense is intended is an even greater fool, for he has succumbed to the will of his adversary.

– Brigham Young

At some point in a meeting, at least one participant is going to make things difficult for you. Most of the time they aren't intentionally trying to do so; nevertheless, their behavior is presenting difficulty to your meeting. Deny the urge to simply resist these participants. Instead, welcome and appreciate them; help them channel their energy in a productive way.

When tensions run high and unfriendly remarks are made, present an opportunity for the participant to reexpress themselves in a more constructive fashion. People will often self-correct inappropriate behavior if it is addressed and they are given the chance to try again.

Here are common difficult behaviors, and our recommendations for language to channel their energy like a Jedi.

Things to say when someone is being difficult

For the critic...

When given negative feedback, especially unsolicited:
"Thank you for pointing this out. How would you suggest that I correct this?"

When they don't want to move on from a disagreement:
"I hear your frustration. In the interest of time, can we move on for now and circle back?"

When they put down input from another participant:
"Hold on, I think he/she/they have a point there."

For the naysayer...

When they are vocal about disagreeing with the consensus, especially when the group has already started work on the subject at hand:

"Is there some way we can solve this problem? What is your view of how we ought to go about this?"

When they object through their body language:

"It seems as though you may have had a reaction to that. Can you help me understand why?"

For the one that doesn't want to be there...

When they enter the space expecting the gathering to be a waste of time:

"You know, I don't think I'd be too excited about wasting my time either. Part of my job is to try to make sure that doesn't happen. So help me a bit here. Why is this going to be a waste of your time?"

When they do not wish to participate:

"We do need your full participation if we can get it. Are we addressing issues that are important to you?

For the one who is frustrated...

When insults, name-calling, or microaggressions occur:

"What did you mean by that?"

When they start putting up a wall:

"Is that the real issue or are you upset about something else?"

When you want to acknowledge their frustration and allow them to speak on it:

"I'm sensing that you are frustrated that _____. Is that how you are feeling or am I wrong?"

When they become uncooperative:

"Is there anything I can say or do at this time to earn your cooperation? I'd sure like to think there is."

For the talker...

When they are too long-winded:

"We are starting to run up on time, can you quickly summarize your thoughts?"

When they are dominating the conversation:

"I'd like to invite the group to share their thoughts on that."

| 5.2 | **Three Ways Jedi Facilitators Get Meetings Back on Track** |

How we say something can often be more important than what we say.

As facilitators, we don't know what is going to come at us. In any meeting, there can be unpredictable moments of stress and conflict. Those are the moments where we must stay steady and graceful.

We have to earn the trust of each participant. Your overall mindset should be to see nobody in the meeting as an enemy or threat.

> For each participant, we have to be a guide on the side rather than a sage on a stage.

You are going to be dealing with derailed meetings. Here are three ways to get the meeting back on track.

METHOD 1 ASK BETTER QUESTIONS

Ask how you can help. Through active listening, we can be responsive instead of reactive. We can show the participant that we are on their team by asking clarifying questions. We like to start with a question for the entire room: "Given what just happened, what are we experiencing right this second?" Remind your group that your only skin in the game is to capture the room intelligence. So if somebody starts going crazy in the meeting, don't shame them. Rather, make use of that moment and ask them how you can help.

If your participant is hesitant or struggling to express themselves, try using these phrases:

Go ahead; I'm all ears.

I can see you're having a hard time putting this into words. That's okay. Keep trying. You're doing great.

I know exactly what you're talking about.

Take your time.

How does that make you feel?

Most of the time participants just want to feel heard, and you can do that by asking clarifying questions. Try to keep asking until you expose what's relevant for the meeting's purpose. Once you uncover their kernel of wisdom, ask how you can capture it for the team. You may find a new perspective that is helpful to the project, and at the very least you will have made a participant feel heard and included. Remember, nobody in the room is your enemy. You are there to guide them to a shared understanding.

METHOD 2 **TAKE A BREAK**

Invite a break. If tension is rising and you feel the activity is not going as planned, you can ask the team if they would like to take a quick break, perhaps asking, "Would a break be helpful right now?" Again, this helps participants feel safe and guided; you are using Jedi force rather than power. A break can provide a chance for people to reset physically as well as mentally, and you can use it as an opportunity to remind people of why they are there. Breaks also provide people who disagree or are interested in exploring something off-topic with an opportunity to have a productive offline discussion without distracting the rest of the meeting participants.

METHOD 3 **PULL PEOPLE ASIDE**

Pulling someone aside during a break. If you are noticing a particular person who is not participating well in the meeting or is clearly agitated, you can pull them aside and ask them whether they are finding value in this meeting. Remind them of the purpose, narrative, and objective. Then ask them if they want to be there and what you can do to make their experience better. Let them know you are there for them and that you would love for them to participate because you value their perspective. If they are dubious of the meeting's goals, remind them that this type of perspective is valuable because it can help the team be more aware of issues. Invite them to join you in asking good questions rather than shooting everything down.

| 5.3 | **How to Sense the Room Dynamic** |

To facilitate from a place of deeper wisdom, you must take the responsibility of sensing the room and creating safety in your group's dynamics.

You need to know how to read participation online versus in person. In person, we can easily tell whether somebody is doing an activity or not. Either they are engaged in the steps that you have laid out and usually have a few clarifying questions about the exercise, or they are obviously participating in some other activity, such as tapping away at their smartphones.

> Remember, if everyone isn't totally engaged, then you are not being a Magical Meeting Jedi.

You need to give each person something to do; otherwise, they will have no real connection to or sense of ownership with the outcomes.

When we are online, we make sure to create activities that give each person their own workspace to create in. This allows you to gauge whether they are participating or not. Using a group sticky wall, it is much harder to notice individual participation levels. When each participant has a digital workspace with their name on it, it becomes obvious who has stopped contributing, as well as who never started in the first place.

We built Control Room, a virtual facilitation tool, to help us with this. We can see when participants are doing an activity and we can call them out if they aren't. Without that visibility, it is hard to assist and provide guidance.

Meeting Jedis cultivate focused participation. If our participants are not paying attention in our meeting, it is as though they never showed up at all. If you call a meeting, you are a facilitator, and you must also call the ground rules. This is a must for attention management.

Our favorite method is to acknowledge that at some point, people may lose focus and become distracted. We instruct them to select a word to use when this occurs. If you were not paying attention because you were on your phone or in another browser tab and you are lost because of it, you simply say a fun word that means you were distracted. For example, we have used "jellyfish" and "puppy." So if you call on a participant and they weren't paying attention, and they are suddenly surprised and have no idea what is going on, they would say "puppy." It allows the person to own that they were distracted; the facilitator can bring them back on track, and everyone else is reminded in a playful way that it is important to pay attention.

With all of these tips above, you can be gracefully firm without being aggressive. Don't meet a lightsaber with a lightsaber. Instead, use constructive Jedi language and get participants back on track with a yielding grace.

| 5.4 | ## How to Facilitate a Group Larger Than Seven People |

How do these principles apply to larger summits or groups that defy the two-pizza rule (a team of more than seven that takes more than two pizzas to feed them)?

If you are planning or facilitating a large summit or meeting, first avoid thinking about it as a gathering of an intimidating number of people.

> Treat your large gathering as a collection of cohorts and small teams.

If your summit is 200 people, focus on creating 20 breakout groups of 10 or 40 groups of five. This approach will change your meeting narrative and the design of certain activities. You can bring facilitators or table leads for each team or let the teams self-manage. If they are self-managing, be sure to share the ground rules and activity instructions just as you would in any small-team meeting. And make sure the ground rules and instructions are visible to everyone at all times.

Also ensure that you have ways to gauge participation. Each person will need a mechanism to participate and capture their team's output. Visit with each group periodically to ensure everyone is on track.

'When did you last eat green vegetables?'

If the cohorts are self-managed, provide them with a simple mechanism to select a table facilitator. It could be the person who most recently ate green vegetables or the person with the longest hair, or maybe something related to your purpose. Simple and fast is key. The table facilitator will keep time at their table, point out when someone is dominating the contributions, etc. Encourage them to get your attention if they are stuck or unsure of what to do next.

| 5.5 | **How to Unlock the Child's Mind in Your Participants** |

Being active, present, and curious creates a fruitful foundation for discovery and productivity. Embrace the child's mind. We all still have an inner child; we just need to access it.

> *When we treat children's play as seriously as* 99
> *it deserves, we are helping them to feel the joy*
> *that's to be found in the creative spirit. It's the*
> *things we play with and the people who help us*
> *play that make a great difference in our lives.*
>
> – Mr. Rogers

As professionals, we usually focus on nouns more than we do verbs. Our adult mind likes to think about work as a series of tasks and a list of set expectations. This limits our creativity to inside-the-box thinking. Children, however, focus on the process.

Focus on verbs rather than nouns to unlock the inner child's mind.

The adult mind is focused on the castle, while the child's mind is focused on the building of said castle. When a child builds a sandcastle, they don't set out to fulfill a rigid ideal of what a sandcastle should be—how many doors it needs, what shape it needs to be, what materials they have to use. When a child builds a sandcastle, they take joy in the process. They unleash their creativity as they go. They decide they need a big backyard for the princess's dragon to play in and a tiny room inside for the mice to live. They see the ocean and decide that the entire interior of the castle actually needs to be filled with water because, as it turns out, the princess is a mermaid.

Play is crucial to harnessing your child's mind; we play because it is joyful, not because we're in pursuit of a goal. When we play, we are focused on the activity at hand, which makes us better able to channel our creativity. When we shift our focus from the nouns to the verbs, constraints evaporate and new opportunities surface.

Besides being creatively freeing, play is fun, and people who have a lot of fun are happier. Employees who enjoy their work are more successful, they are more productive and more relaxed, they collaborate better and communicate more effectively.

What would a five-year old do?
→

When play is incorporated in work culture, a safe space is opened to fail fearlessly and to make room for marvel instead of judgment. You can integrate improv activities or deploy many of the exercises we mention in Chapters 3.1 and 3.4 to free participants from stifling seriousness.

To form more connection and open minds

We recommend using provocative questions to shift how particpants introduce themselves to one another. So one question we often ask in a session either in person or virtual is:

"Introduce yourself by telling us about a moment in your life when you felt daring."

People come up with all sorts of things, from skydiving to standing up to their overbearing aunt. The stories are amazing, but more importantly, remembering them puts everyone emotionally back into that moment of their lives. This is a great mindset from which to get them contributing and engaging.

A few other questions that help open minds:

· Tell us your best scary story

· What superhero best symbolizes you?

· What do you do in your free time that gives you a lot of meaning?

| 5.6 | **Great Facilitators Don't Need All the Answers** |

When I give up trying to impress the group, I become very impressive. Let go in order to achieve. The wise facilitator speaks rarely and briefly, teaching more through being than doing.

– The Tao Te Ching

Just like a great Jedi, you do not need all the answers. Use your intuition. Use the Force, be flexible and allow participant enthusiasm to steer your meeting.

If a few participants are starting to self-form a task force in the meeting to knock out one of the activities and you had not planned on that happening, it is ok for you to let go of control for a while. If their self-forming is in the service of the purpose, let it unfold and make sure to capture their combined genius.

> If the enthusiasm in the room is high and everyone is engaged, lean back and let it happen.

We jokingly say this is the best facilitator Jedi move because it allows you to do less! If you have done the prep work, set the ground rules, and made each participant's contribution clear, most other things tend to take care of themselves. This is how you use the Force to be a lazy facilitator.

Always look for ways to distribute control in your meeting. Protect the purpose, be focused on the objective and facilitate the room intelligence. If the group starts steering out of enthusiasm and excitement, let it unfold naturally while you sit back and enjoy observing the collaboration. Don't get in the way of wonderful team dynamics when they happen. Your job is to provide the scaffolding for that to occur.

CHAPTER SUMMARY
KEY TAKEAWAYS:

- Use Jedi language to create a positive situation when a participant is being difficult.

- Focus on verbs rather than nouns to tap into the child's mind.

- Treat a large gathering as a collection of cohorts and small teams.

- Include everyone in your activities or risk losing their attention.

- You can be a lazy facilitator; if participants are taking positive control and you are staying on time, let it happen.

CHAPTER 6

Using Feedback Effectively (And Making It Fun)

Meetings are not only an opportunity to extract and capture room intelligence for the project, but they are also a chance to upgrade your culture even when things are going great.

6.1 Debriefs Aren't Just for Bad Outcomes

Retrospectives and debriefs are obvious when something goes wrong. We usually have an intentional debrief only after a terrible meeting or a failed project.

When you have a magical meeting, it's easy to rest on your laurels and forget about feedback. What do we need to reflect on if everything goes well?

Intentional debriefings will help guarantee that meetings stay magical.

At the closing of your magical meeting, ask the group questions such as:

Feedback: Magical Questions to Ask

- What are you proud of from this meeting? What made this gathering so great?

- If we did this meeting again, what would you change?

- What other opportunities and problems in our company could benefit from a meeting like this?

- What are the takeaway lessons from this activity?

- What were the strengths and weaknesses of today's session/this workshop?

- What is something bold that you might do after leaving this room?

When we debrief after a great meeting, we have a chance to socialize awesome meeting behavior. Everyone gets an opportunity to gain the wisdom of the facilitator. Otherwise, you are the only one leaving the meeting knowing what made it magical. It is obvious to you, but it isn't obvious to your participants. Focusing on what works allows us to repeat that success; in addition, sometimes we uncover patterns that we can use elsewhere.

| 6.2 | **Making Feedback Fun** |

Feedback can be brutal sometimes. But if you design it into your meeting, it can take the sting away. When you collect feedback during the meeting rather than waiting until afterward, participants are more likely to share and remember critical details. You can also use live feedback to elaborate on details that might be lost in a survey.

This is also an opportunity to demonstrate that you care. Listen carefully, ask clarifying questions, and thank people for their feedback. As Douglas Stone and Sheila Heen advise in their book *Thanks For The Feedback*, "People won't give you feedback until they think you actually want it."

Treat feedback as a gift. ←

According to Stone and Heen, for feedback to be effective and not damaging to our ego, it needs to incorporate evaluation, coaching and appreciation. That is why we are fans of using "Rose

Thorn Bud" "Plus Delta," and "It Made Me Think" for capturing feedback in our workshops.

Feedback: The Rose Thorn Bud

Give each participant stickies of different colors

> Rose = Things that are positive go on pink stickies
> Thorn = Things that are negative go on blue stickies
> Bud = Things that have potential go on green stickies

Have each participant silently generate as many roses, thorns, and buds as possible. Instruct them only include one issue, idea or insight per Post-it. Have them select one rose, one thorn, and one bud to share with the group. Listen carefully and take notes.

Feedback: Plus Delta

Pluses are appreciative elements the participant enjoyed and wants to see more of.

Deltas are coaching moments of improvement and/or elements they wish the meeting or workshop would have provided.

You can treat the exercise the same as Rose Thorn Bud, but with less stickies since there are only 2 topic areas.

Feedback: It Made Me Think

At the end of the meeting, participants will go around in a circle sharing an insight, discovery, question, or challenge that really struck them, following the format:

> "_____;
> it made me think."

The idea is to boil down their biggest takeaway into a single, brief sentence. This activity will give you valuable feedback on how (and if!) the discussions of the day succeeded in getting participants to think differently or more deeply about the topics or questions posed.

If everyone seems to have the same answer, consider diversifying your next meeting; this could mean inviting team members from different backgrounds, departments, experience levels, or social circles.

These are solid feedback frameworks because they incorporate evaluation, coaching, and appreciation rather than just evaluation.

The evaluation components let you know where you currently stand. The coaching components give you a clear path for leveling up. The appreciation components warm our hearts and remind us why it matters to be a facilitator. All of these types of feedback combined enable growth and leave you inspired rather than triggered by only negative feedback. It also shows others that receiving feedback doesn't have to suck.

As Navy Seal and best-selling author Jocko Willink says, "A leader must be humble but not passive; quiet but not silent."[4]

When we implement feedback into our meeting, we show up humble and can even invite a bit of humor. We help the entire room embody the growth mindset. Make fun feedback a core part of your agenda with the methods above. We love ending our workshops with "Rose Thorn Bud" because it reminds everyone that there is always room for improvement, even after a magical meeting.

6.3 Exactly What to Say When the Situation Gets Hard

You know those moments in a meeting where it's uncomfortable but nobody wants to address it? Those are the moments where it usually gets quiet and everyone is looking at each other and looking at you wondering, "What do we do now?" This is usually during a moment when an uncomfortable topic or conflict arises.

Let's consider an uncomfortable topic for many people: racism. White men have have been actively learning how to keep the difficult topic of racism top of mind and properly hold space for conversations involving race and racism.

> Diversity and inclusion goes beyond having a diverse set of participants.

One book that has helped us mature as facilitators is Robin DiAngelo's *White Fragility*. DiAngelo talks about "silence breakers," and they have been a powerful method for us to incorporate more feedback into our workshops. They are wonderful because they allow the facilitator to appear vulnerable and also encourage others to be vulnerable.

Don't be afraid to break the silence. →

Silence breakers enable curiosity and humility in difficult moments and conversation. You can use them to expand, rather than ignore, discussion and connection.

Here are a few Silence Breakers we have remixed from DiAngelo's work to keep top of mind in all meetings. These allow for deep, diverse, and meaningful feedback to preserve dignity in meetings.

Silence Breakers

When you sense a shift in energy in the room, you can say "I just felt something shift in the room. I'm wondering if anyone else did?"

If you notice a few people have a negative nonverbal reaction to something, you can say "It seems as though some people may have had a reaction to that. Can you help me understand why?"

If you find yourself enthusiastic about something and the room isn't matching your enthusiasm, you can invite "Can you help me understand whether what I'm thinking right now might be problematic?"

After listening to someone talk about something difficult and you want to make sure you fully understand their perspective, you can say "This is what I understand you to be saying: ____ Is that accurate?"

When others seem to passively disagree but are not engaging in discussion, you can say "I'm hearing a passive 'yeah but' or a 'it's fine.' Can you help me work through it with you?"

When someone says something offensive or displays some other form of microaggression, you can say "What did you mean by that?"

When awkward moments present themselves, be brave and vulnerable and allow the moment of silence to become a moment of human growth and inclusion. Use these silence-breaker questions to lead the group into deeper conversations and forms of evolving feedback.

CHAPTER SUMMARY
KEY TAKEAWAYS:

- In a moment of conflict, default to asking questions, calmly.

- Nobody in your meeting is a threat (usually!); remember that participants might be opponents sometimes, but they are not enemies.

- Don't wait for feedback after the meeting to make adjustments; incorporate fun feedback activities into the meeting so everyone has the opportunity to empathize and level up.

- It is OK to let enthusiastic participants steer the meeting at certain moments; loose facilitation works.

- Use silence breakers to create grace during difficult conversations.

CHAPTER 7

How to Be a Magical Meeting Participant

Meetings are nothing without participation. No matter how incredible a facilitator may be, a meeting will not be successful without the input of its participants. You have power as a participant; here are some ways you can use it wisely.

7.1 Recognize the Facilitator's Perspective: The entire forest vs. a single tree

Before you enter the meeting space, do your best to understand the context of the facilitator's objective. Will you be discussing nuts and bolts or big ideas? Should you be ready to discuss the entire forest or focus on a single tree?

Understanding the purpose and objective of the meeting will help you get aligned with others. A meeting about tactics will require you to think more granularly than a meeting about vision or strategy. A meeting focused on problem-solving requires a different approach than a meeting to decide how to completely undo a big decision from the past that isn't working out. In a meeting about vision and big picture, being caught up in small details and implementation tactics will slow the room down and bog down everyone's creativity. On the flip side, dreaming big in a meeting about gritty details will waste time and frustrate other attendees who are trying to drill in deeper.

Consider who called the meeting. Is this person a maker or a manager, an executive or a developer? Does this person's role dispose them to focusing on the big picture or the finer details? The creative director might appreciate a sky-is-the-limit attitude, but the head engineer might be frustrated by a lack of realism. If you're having trouble discerning how close to the ground or high in the air you should expect to operate, communicate this.

Before the meeting, approach other attendees, your team lead, or even the facilitator. If other attendees also feel unclear about expectations, meet with the facilitator and bring it to their attention. If you are unable to do so ahead of time, find a chance to ask for more clarity toward the beginning of the meeting.

Always come to a meeting with some kind of prototype. Be prepared with a visual artifact of some kind. Either ask the facilitator what could be useful or make a guess based on the meeting title and description. Then you can create a rough draft, quick sketch, or outline to bring in as a prototype.

If the room is struggling, you can introduce your prototype as a starting point for gathering everyone's ideas and opinions. At the very least, it will help you unambiguously explore the meeting's purpose and set the proper altitude.

> If you're unable to create a prototype before the meeting, consider not attending.

If you aren't in the headspace to contribute strategy for a meeting on strategy, the best thing you can do is bench yourself. If you decide the meeting would be best without you, let the organizer know that you'll be sitting this one out. Thank them for considering you and, if appropriate, suggest someone else who might be a better fit.

7.2   Be a Partner to the Facilitator

Good facilitators know how to ask the right questions because they're constantly on the lookout for a lack of alignment, but even awesome facilitators have blind spots. When you see something the facilitator is missing, help them see it by asking the right questions.

Listen for inconsistency

Sometimes it may seem that two people are aligned even when they are not; Person A and Person B may think they are saying the same thing but in fact be saying very different things. On the flip side, two people may argue when they don't understand that they're saying the exact same thing.

If this happens and the facilitator doesn't catch it, ask provocative questions to help Person A and Person B uncover the lack of alignment for themselves. It can be helpful to repeat what Person A is saying in Person B's language and vice versa. A good facilitator will catch on to what you've noticed and run with it.

> If you have relevant knowledge, insight or a perspective that no one else is sharing, frame it as a question.

Questions have two superpowers. First, they avoid triggering defensiveness in others because they come across more gently than "telling it like it is." Second, they give you room to be wrong. If you have a misunderstanding or are just plain wrong about something and you share in the form of a question, it is easy for someone to correct you and provide the room with better information. Incorrect, misinformed or misunderstood information as a statement of fact requires much more courage to correct.

The most important rule of improv is to always say "Yes, and?" It is critical to hear your scene partner, incorporate their contributions, and then give them more to work with. Good questions operate in meetings much the same way that "Yes, and?" operates in improv: They tell other participants that you hear them and understand them, giving them more to work with rather than ending the conversation.

In order to "Yes, and?" other participants using good questions, you need to first listen. What are most people thinking about during a meeting? The next thing they're about to say. There are a lot of reasons people do this, but most of them boil down to this: they don't want to sound stupid. Rather than say something that others might judge them for, they sit nervously and perfectly prepare the best thing to say and the best way to say it.

The irony is that this leads to worse responses rather than better ones; by not listening to what others are sharing, we're limiting the value of the insight or feedback that we can share. Listen to the other participants. Your responses do not need to be fully rehearsed, Pulitzer Prize–worthy prose. They do, however, need to consider or incorporate the insights shared by others in the room. Relax and listen.

Part of being a friend to the facilitator is allowing them to lead the flow of the meeting. If you want to ask a question about logistics, share something or introduce a new idea and you don't know if it's an appropriate time to do so, ask!

THE NON-OBVIOUS GUIDE TO MAGICAL MEETINGS

> "Is this an appropriate time for me to _____?" is a very simple question that will help keep the meeting on time and on task.

It is likely that if the answer is no, the facilitator will return to you when the appropriate time comes. If you notice that things are dragging or going completely off the rails, help the facilitator by giving this feedback in the form of a question: "I notice that we're a little off task here. How can we get this back on track?"

Pro tip: Asking "Why?" can put people on the defensive. Consider reframing the question: Instead of asking, "Why do you like this idea?" you could ask, "What about this idea do you like?"

If the meeting is large, you do not know the facilitator or how they respond to feedback, or there isn't enough trust in the room for you to feel comfortable providing this feedback publicly, you could ask for a break. During the break, approach the facilitator and ask how you can help keep the meeting on track.

> The goal is to be an ally rather than throw the facilitator under the bus.

Questions aren't the only way to be a friend to the facilitator. Step up when you see tasks that may be falling through the cracks. If it feels as though the facilitator is having trouble capturing room intelligence and no one is scribing, offer to jump up to the white board.

PRO TIP FOR SCRIBING

Even if something seems obvious, restate it aloud to be sure that both you and the room are clear on the information you're recording. If a meeting is coming to a close and the next steps aren't clear, request a debrief. Have the facilitator or team leader lay out who is responsible for what and when/if there will be a follow-up meeting.

Overall, find opportunities to assist the facilitator before the meeting even begins. Are you nearing the date of the meeting and haven't received an agenda? Offer to make one. Is the organizer in the process of inviting participants? Offer to help get the word out. Just because you are a participant rather than a facilitator or the organizer doesn't mean you have to sit back and be passive. Take the bull by the horns!

| 7.3 | **Silence Denotes Agreement: The impact of what you don't say** |

Understand that silence has an impact. When you say nothing, you are telling the room that you are in agreement with what someone is saying. Do not say nothing while a decision you disagree with is being made. Do not wait until after a meeting is over to approach the facilitator or organizer about your disagreement. If you disagree with a discussion or a decision being made during a meeting, speak up. That is what the meeting is for.

> Remember that great meetings come to a consensus, not necessarily unanimous agreement.

Not everyone will love a decision, and that's ok; it is still important, however, to speak up. Perhaps you disagree because of a factor or perspective that others have not yet considered, or maybe others feel the same as you but are nervous to be the first to disagree.

Consider the blast radius of the decision you're not in agreement with. How much pain or cost will be associated with reversing the decision should that be necessary? How much damage could the decision do in and of itself? Is this a pebble being thrown into a pool or a 300-pound football player doing a cannonball into one? If the decision is minor, it is enough to voice your opinion and let the room move on. If it is major, it may be worth pushing back a little harder. Find the right balance between shutting the room down and sitting quietly while you aren't in agreement with it.

Perhaps you're not in disagreement at all; rather, you have an alternative idea or you're just straight-up confused.

> A good facilitator will read the room and help everyone stay on the same page, but it is your responsibility as a participant to speak up if you're behind or need help.

Silence implies agreement, and agreement implies understanding. Speak up and help the facilitator help you.

CHAPTER SUMMARY
KEY TAKEAWAYS:

- Check the perspective and context of the meeting you are attending.

- Help the facilitator with questions.

- Don't be silent if you are confused or have a problem.

- Feedback, next steps and accountability are gold for all participants; request them before the meeting is over.

PART THREE

After Your Meetings and Your Meeting Culture

CHAPTER 8

Sharing the Meeting Story

Ok. You facilitated an amazing meeting. The job is done, right? Not so fast ...

The question "If a tree falls in a forest and no one is around to hear it, does it make a sound?" is a philosophical thought experiment that raises opinions about observation and perception. In the context of meeting culture, we remix that line to, "If an awesome meeting occurred and nobody else at the company knows about it, did it actually happen?" In most cases, we have come to realize the answer to that is no. A magical meeting leads to some kind of progress and change, and those not in attendance need to be brought up to speed somehow.

Not everyone can attend your meeting, so how do you inform those who could not attend about the progress that was made?

For a magical meeting to reach its full potential, the facilitator must treat it like a director and editor would treat the production of a movie.

Each participant is a guardian of change that you can enlist to accurately spread the magical meeting's outcomes throughout the organization.

8.1 The Magical Meeting Story Spine

After your meeting, you need to share a narrative for others to understand the meeting's effectiveness and outcomes. This way, you can keep up momentum and avoid project slumps. And at the heart of an amazing narrative is the story spine.

The story spine is a technique from improv theater created by Kenn Adams, author of *How to Improvise a Full Length Play: The Art of Spontaneous Theater*. It was popularized for storytelling by Pixar story artist Emma Coats' tweets on Pixar's "22 Rules of Storytelling."

The story spine follows a very structured formula so you can focus on the details, not the sentence or order. Think of each step as a sentence-starter to help you rough out your story.

Once upon a time there was [___].

Every day, [___].

One day [___].

Because of that, [___].

Because of that, [___]. (and so on)

Until finally [___].

And every day after that [___].

We recommend using the story spine in most of your communication strategy. It is a great way to pitch a new product or communicate customer empathy. But the usual template isn't perfect for magical meetings, so we have remixed it a bit for the context of an effective meeting. We call it the Magical Meeting Story Spine.

The Magical Meeting Story Spine

Before our meeting, there was...
[a problem or opportunity].

So we had a meeting/workshop to...
[drive an outcome for that problem or opportunity].

As a team we,
[did these activities].

Because of that, we made...
[these decisions].

Because of that, we now have...
[this potential].

If you want to look over our work, you can review our artifacts...
[in this archive].

Moving forward, we are focused on...
[this momentum].

If you have questions or concerns, you can contact...
[the decider or facilitator].

Use the magical meeting story spine as the starting point for sharing your magical meeting's purpose, outcomes and next steps.

The following sections will help you fill in the magical meeting story spine with confidence.

| 8.2 | **You Captured; Now Curate the Highlight Reel** |

As we mentioned in Chapter 4.4, a great facilitator is proactively capturing the room intelligence of discussions and decisions that are being made by the meeting participants. This could be on a whiteboard or using a digital design board tool such as MURAL. The output of your meeting needs to be highly visual. If you did good work in the meeting, you will have something to show for it.

> You are developing a library of artifacts that begins to have a positive compounding effect on your meeting culture.

After the meeting, just like the team at ESPN, it's time to make your highlight reel. Show your stakeholders the touchdowns, a few of the amazing plays, and the final score breakdown. This is essential for creating a shared understanding across your organization so you don't lose momentum.

Think about it as a video memo. →

Make a short recap video that highlights the moments you are proud of as the facilitator. What visuals did the team create that best summarize the amazing work that was done in the meeting? Capture them with your smartphone or screen-recording tool of choice.

Make compelling presentations using the assets you captured. With video, you can showcase the artifacts that were created and explain why they matter.

In the magical meeting story spine we shared above, this video should especially speak to the following parts:

As a team we
[did these activities].

Because of that, we made...
[these decisions].

Because of that, we now have...
[this potential].

Your video could be links that fit in those brackets or you could make an entire video that fills in the story spine.

We record a screen-share video of us walking through the key digital artifacts that were created, explaining how we made decisions and discussing the key alignment and commitments moving forward. It is important to embody the advice and show rather than tell.

> Ideally your highlight reel should be visual. Don't just send an email with bullet points. Have fun with it!

8.3 Share Your Highlights Archive

In the magical meeting story spine, there is a powerful section to help empower more asynchronous work and trust within your organization:

> *If you want to look over our work, you can review our artifacts...*
> *[in this archive].*

In all of your meeting follow-ups, link to the captures archive you created with the meeting's key artifacts.

If you don't have any artifacts to show, the magical meeting didn't happen.

We have found that if you are consistent in sharing the artifacts from meetings, you can help alleviate one of the biggest problems in meeting culture: people attending meetings because of fear of missing out (FOMO). Once outsiders are able to easily appreciate and access the work that was done in the meeting, they can feel less stressed out about not being involved in every meeting.

Digital collaboration boards are still handy for in-person workshops. →

Even with in-person meetings, rather than take photos we like to use a virtual whiteboard tool such as MURAL. You can workshop and do activities with analog tools and materials, but we digitize the main artifacts and findings inside a digital whiteboard. Digital tools also allow us to export data for different styles of analysis, whereas photos are more limited. Durability is also a concern because the physical room you are in will likely need to be cleaned after your meeting.

You can take all the photos of stickies you want, but if you don't make sense of them in some meaningful layout and design, then no story emerges. If you have a digital replica of the room inside of a MURAL, you have an archive in the cloud, allowing all meeting participants to easily reference, remix, clone and share the magical work that was done.

With this, you can build a magical meetings archive. With an ongoing archive of digital meeting boards, you can empower the wonderful behavior of sharing the work that was done in a meeting asynchronously. Using these interactive design boards not only tells the story of the great work done in the meeting, it showcases what a magical meeting looks like and helps remind others that a solid meeting is much more than just an agenda or a list of talking points.

| 8.4 | **Formats for Your Stories** |

There are many methods for how you might tell your meeting story.

You could have each participant give you a quote summarizing what the outcome of the meeting was and create a collage of these quotes, then share a photo of the collage with the rest of the team or company.

Maybe someone on the team is a talented illustrator and jotted down graphics of highlights from the meeting. If so, share that!

You could also interview one of the meeting participants in a podcast-like format and share that conversation with others on the team, giving them a conversational recap of the meeting and general facilitation tips.

CHAPTER SUMMARY
KEY TAKEAWAYS:

- Use the Magical Meeting Story Spine to empower participants with an accurate and powerful story.

- Create an entertaining highlight reel of the meeting outcomes.

- Remember: Most people skim content, so it is your job to curate the most meaningful updates from your magical meeting.

CHAPTER 9

How to Inspire Good Meeting Culture

Whether you're being intentional about it or not, your meeting practices are creating a meeting culture that sculpts your team's behavior, expectations and attitudes. To get the most out of your meetings, take control of your organization's meeting culture.

9.1 Update Your Meeting Culture Constantly

Your meeting culture is like the early release of an smart-phone app: It might work, but there are probably bugs that could be improved.

The way you meet needs updates, just as the devices in our pockets do.

The founders of Basecamp and authors of *It Doesn't Have To Be Crazy at Work,* Jason Fried and David Heinemeier Hansson, have a helpful way for leaders to think about making their company more calm:

"When you start to think about your company as a product, all sorts of new possibilities for improvement emerge. When you realize the way you work is malleable, you can start molding something new, something better. We work on our company as hard as we work on our products."

Design the way you want to work. →

If you are aware of habits and expectations bugging your culture and leading to unnecessary stress, it's time to upgrade your company's culture.

First, you'll need to identify your bugs. We use Triz, an awesome exercise developed by the Liberating Structures community to do this.

Triz

1. Make a list of all you can do to make sure that you achieve the worst meeting possible.

2. Go down this list item by item and ask yourselves, "Is there anything that we are currently doing that in any way, shape, or form resembles this item?" Be brutally honest to make a second list of all your counterproductive activities/programs/procedures.

3. Go through the items on your second list and decide what first steps will help you stop what you know creates undesirable results.

Often, people are nervous to bring up the bugs of their meeting culture. Using Triz makes it possible to speak the unspeakable and get skeletons out of the closet.

All of the feedback and growth methods in this chapter so far will help you spot the bugs in your culture. Next question: How do you fix them?

9.2 Lessons Identified vs. Lessons Learned

Using Triz or a similar method, you can build a list of lessons identified—but they are not learned yet. Let's explore the difference.

Lessons identified are observations, insights, and feedback you've recorded about how to improve the way you run meetings. And while it may feel cathartic to uncover all this gold, you can't stop there. To create lessons learned, you must actually put a new practice in place.

Our advice is to keep a running checklist of the lessons identified and then workshop how they will be applied.

> Lessons must be accompanied by actions if they are to be considered learned.

You must put in place a new procedure, policy, framework, or mantra, then communicate this meeting-culture software update to your team members so working practices can be changed. If nothing changes, nothing was learned.

For example, we once had a lesson identified that many people felt some of the meetings they were invited to were not relevant to them. As a result, we created a meeting mantra of "All meetings are optional."

Although this might be seen as scandalous at other companies, it has been wonderful for us. If a team member doesn't think they need to attend a meeting, they're free to decline it. It's a small gesture, but a reflection of our belief that many meetings just don't need to happen. This policy has led to an increase in quick and direct conversations and ultimately to fewer meetings and more space and time for the things we want (and need) to do. With this mantra in practice, we have taken the lesson identified and made it learned.

You don't have to go to every meeting.
←

What meeting mantra could you make to improve your meeting culture?

| 9.3 | **Meeting Debt: Building a repository of meetings** |

Unless you're an actual, real-life superhero, you've experienced work debt. At some point, you've fallen into the trap of thinking, "We'll save this project for later" or "We'll fix this when we have more time." The procrastination accumulates until you're finally forced to deal with all of the projects and tasks that you've been putting off; then, instead of chipping away at the problem a little bit at a time, you have to climb an entire mountain in much too little time. This might have caused you to cut corners or produce less quality work than you would have liked. Meeting debt works much the same way.

> Meeting debt is an accumulation of unchecked meetings and habits that have resulted in a meeting culture that doesn't work, and may even be toxic.

One bad meeting may frustrate some team members; five bad meetings might make team members dread your meetings; 20 bad meetings might set a precedent for apathy and pessimism across your entire office. Meeting systems that have built up a lot of meeting debt waste time, money, and the strengths of your team.

Meeting debt, however, is not a death sentence. If you do the work to fix your meeting system, you can begin to pay off your meeting debt. To do this, you'll need to develop a repository of meetings.

A repository of meetings is a record of the meetings you've held in the past—what were the objectives, how did they go, and what were the outcomes? Recording the objectives should be easy, as there shouldn't be any meetings called without a purpose; if you find that you've held a lot of meetings without a clear objective, that is a critical bit of information to take note of. When considering how well (or badly!) your meetings have gone, there are a handful of questions you can ask yourself.

→ What percentage of attendees took an active role in participating?

→ How effectively were participants able to communicate?

→ What did you and the participants learn/discover? What did you want to learn/discover but did not?

→ Were the right people invited to the meeting? Who didn't need to be there? Who should have been there but was not invited?

→ What kind of feedback did you receive after the meeting? (If you haven't been asking for feedback, start working feedback activities into your agendas!)

→ How many lessons identified did your retrospection generate?

→ Most importantly: Did the meeting fulfill your objective?

To determine the outcome of your meeting, consider both your original objective and what your participants do after the meeting is over. Your outcome may be new tasks or assignments that are completed, projects that are started, challenges that are overcome, or new skills or knowledge obtained. How did your meeting create change?

9.4   How to Use Your Repository to Design a New Meeting System

Once you've built a repository of meetings, it's time to begin auditing. Figure out which meetings are working for you, which ones are not, and which ones have promise but aren't quite working yet. Once you've done this, you can begin intentionally designing a new meeting system with clearly defined types of meetings, how they will work, and when it will be appropriate to use them.

Steps To Design a New Meeting System

✓ Sort Your Meetings

✓ Reflect on Meeting Quality

✓ Segment by Meeting Type

✓ Redesign Your Meeting Templates

✓ Create a Flowchart or Diagram for Your Effective Meetings

STEP 1 **SORT YOUR MEETINGS**

The first thing you should do is compare your meetings' objectives to their outcomes. This will help you sort them into groups based on their success (working, not working, or has potential). It will usually be very clear whether a meeting fulfilled its objective or not, but sometimes there may be a bit of a grey area.

Perhaps you held a meeting to create a new piece of print material; by the end of the meeting, your team completed the design, but the print material was never distributed. In a situation such as this, you'll have to reflect on where the ball was dropped. At the end of the meeting, did you fail to clearly articulate who was responsible for each next step? Did an issue with the printer arise later in the process, completely out of your control? If the issue could have been solved within your meeting, put this one in the "has potential" pile; if nothing that you could have done during the meeting would have prevented the issue, you're probably safe to put it in the "working" pile.

STEP 2 **REFLECT ON MEETING QUALITY**

Once you have your meetings sorted, it's time to get into the meat of meetings. This will require some critical thinking and self-reflection. Pile by pile, go through the meetings and take a look at what you've recorded for "How the meeting went." Which activities worked as intended? Which ones didn't? What could have been done to better harness attitudes or attention in the room? How were participants' individual strengths brought to the table?

You will begin to see patterns emerge. Perhaps problem-solving meetings went really well when participants were broken into small groups, for example.

STEP 3 SEGMENT BY MEETING TYPE

The final step in auditing your past meetings is to separate them out by type of meeting (objectives will be helpful here) and then design meetings for each objective. These categories will look different depending on your workplace and what your team's responsibilities are, but they may include design meetings, problem-solving meetings, innovation meetings, restructuring meetings, etc. Look for more patterns. Review all the meetings in one category and pick out what worked and what didn't work for that type of meeting. This will help you understand how to define your meeting types and decide when they are appropriate.

STEP 4 REDESIGN YOUR MEETING TEMPLATES

Use the information that you've learned analyzing your meetings by type to design a new meeting for each type that you've recognized.

Write a basic agenda for each type of meeting and select a pool of activities that either have worked for your team or seem like they should work for your team to accomplish the objectives of that type of meeting.

Doing this work up front will prevent you from scrambling to start from scratch next time you're organizing a meeting. It will also clearly define for others the purpose of activities in your pool.

STEP 5 CREATE A FLOWCHART OR DIAGRAM FOR YOUR EFFECTIVE MEETINGS

Now that you've done the work to dissect your meeting repository and design your meeting system, it will be helpful to create a flowchart or railroad diagram to clearly illustrate how you will decide when and what type of meetings are appropriate given the purpose, objective, and timing. The diagram will serve as a helpful tool in implementing your new system and help others understand how the system will work so that they can put it into action.

Keep in mind that your new system may not magically change your team's entire meeting culture right away. It may take others a few meetings to adjust (paying off the meeting debt), and as with anything new it may take a little bit of tweaking or editing to perfect. Don't be afraid to try new activities or facilitation techniques, but be sure to return to your repository every now and then to evaluate their effectiveness and where they should be placed in your meeting system.

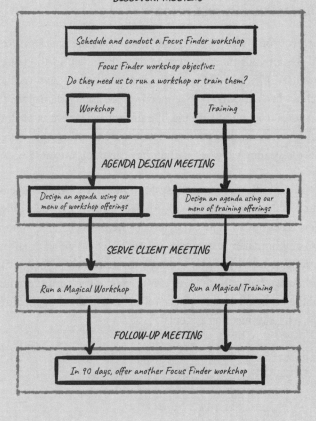

Meeting System Example

Situation: New client interested in working with us

DISCOVERY MEETING

Schedule and conduct a Focus Finder workshop

Focus Finder workshop objective:
Do they need us to run a workshop or train them?

Workshop | Training

AGENDA DESIGN MEETING

Design an agenda using our menu of workshop offerings | Design an agenda using our menu of training offerings

SERVE CLIENT MEETING

Run a Magical Workshop | Run a Magical Training

FOLLOW-UP MEETING

In 90 days, offer another Focus Finder workshop

9.5   Less Is More: The Power of Small Teams

Who you bring to the table is just as important as what you're going to work on. A small team of people who all know why they are in the room and what they can contribute will be much more powerful than a large room of people who are questioning their relevance to the work at hand.

No one likes having their time wasted. If you as the event organizer invite team members who aren't right for the work that you're focusing on, you are wasting their time. This is not good for your meeting culture, their workplace satisfaction, or your company's bottom line. Besides thinking critically about who you want to invite and why, there are two ways you can prevent team members from feeling as though their time isn't valued.

First, tell them exactly why you are inviting them to the meeting and why you think they would be a valuable contribution to the room when you extend the invitation. Second, mention that the meeting is optional. If they decline, you can request that they share why they don't see value in their participation.

> Small teams rock. Smaller teams are able to communicate better, share more of their ideas and better harness the potential of every person in the room.

The more people in a group, the lower the expectation that each individual will need to actively contribute. In a room of 50 people, people social loaf; it is easy to get distracted or fade into the background. In a room of five people, it's nearly impossible. Even if you have great participation, too many participants can lead to chaos. Too many voices in a room will also prevent the team from diving deeply into the ideas presented (there may be time to deep-dive into 10 peoples' thoughts, but there likely isn't time to deep-dive into 100 individual ideas).

9.6 Less Is More: How to Combat FOMO

As you start cutting back on the number of participants in your meetings, some of your team members may experience a bit of FOMO. There are a number of ways to combat this.

If you have a history of large meetings, your first step should be to let everyone know you will be holding smaller meetings. Explain that no one needs panic at not receiving a meeting invite; it does not mean anyone has been deliberately excluded. Share the benefits of meeting with smaller groups and let people know that this change is being made to provide them better conditions in which to do their best work.

Don't hold secret meetings.

Be public about the objective of your meeting and encourage your team members to speak with you if they haven't made the guest list but feel they have something of value to contribute. Team members who are completely irrelevant to the meeting will be glad they weren't asked to attend, and team members who feel they would be right for the meeting will have the opportunity to address this. If you have a team member who feels they are right for every meeting, don't be afraid to ask them to sit a few out. You can thank them for their drive to contribute and let them know that you value their work but want to give the less vocal members of the team a chance to shine.

Support your less active participants. ←

Share links to your meetings archive folder, which we discussed in Chapter 8. This will allow team members who are interested in the work being done but may not be uniquely suited to it (or just don't have the time) to stay informed.

9.7	**Human-Centered Meetings: Using the human-centered design process to improve your meetings**

Meetings, like products, should meet the needs of the team engaging with them. When you're designing your meetings, the human beings who will be attending them should be at the center of your process. Your meeting culture will be infinitely more positive when your team members feel that the meetings they are asked to attend serve them in pursuit of their best work. Let's look at how human-centered design, a design philosophy focused on putting human needs, wants, and desires ahead of everything else, will make your meetings better.

The human-centered design process puts the user—that is, whoever will be engaging with the end product—at the very core of the design process. It explores the needs and desires of the user as well as how designers can best meet those needs and desires. When using this process to design better meetings, your attendees will be your user/consumer. There are six phases to the human-centered design process.

PHASE 1 ENGAGE AND OBSERVE

Apply this phase to engaging with and observing your meeting attendees. Observe the way that your team members behave in meetings to better understand them; this will help you design meetings suited for them. Look for patterns of behavior. Find challenges that team members seem to be facing—perhaps distractions, self-consciousness, communication issues, or something else entirely.

Notice what they do well. Do they do a great job of sharing the spotlight? Are they brilliant at keeping on schedule? Engage with your team. Ask them what feels good about your meetings and what would help them feel even better. This will help you design meetings that will play to your team's strengths and support their weaknesses.

PHASE 2 IDEATION

Generate as many ideas as possible without worrying about the details. Don't get caught in the nitty-gritty of whether each idea will work—or worse, how it will work—as this is a brainstorming phase. Unleash your inner child's mind and put creativity in the driver's seat. Keep your team's needs and desires at the forefront of your mind.

PHASE 3 PROTOTYPING

In product design, this obviously means creating something tangible. For human-centered meetings, you'll be prototyping methods and activities. Perhaps you create a new activity for your team to practice a communication skill they are currently struggling with. Perhaps you find a new, fun way to start your meetings and make everyone feel more relaxed. Maybe you're prototyping logistical components, such as the time of day you're meeting or the size of the space you're meeting in. This stage is not about being perfect. There will be time to refine your prototype, so don't feel pressured to get it right the first time.

PHASE 4 FEEDBACK

Test your meeting prototype on the teammates who attend your meetings. Let them know exactly what need or desire you're aiming to fulfill, and ask them how the prototype either succeeds or fails. Be sure to collect as many details as possible; the more information you have, the better prepared you will be for the next phase.

PHASE 5 INTEGRATION

In this fifth phase, you will review the feedback that you've received and use it to make your prototype better. Perhaps you moved your meetings to the beginning of the workday because your team became easily distracted by other obligations in the afternoon, but you received feedback that team members weren't quite awake and ready to get deep in the morning. Adjust your prototype using this new information, again keeping at the forefront of your mind the team's need or desire that you've decided to tackle. This step may take a few rounds of integration, testing and repeating. Once your solution is the best version of itself (and replicable!), it's time to move on to the final step.

PHASE 6 APPLICATION

Apply your new human-centered meeting tactic. Add your new activity to your activity pool, apply your improved logistics to important meetings—whatever your solution, bring it into your meetings. Keep in mind that teams change, people change, the world changes, and therefore needs change. There may be a day where your solution is no longer serving your team; if this happens, return to phase one and repeat the process. But don't wait around for something to break; run the process on a regular schedule to see what new opportunities surface.

9.8 How to Design Your Own Meeting Mantras

At Voltage Control, we follow 10 meeting mantras in our internal meetings and the meetings we design for clients. They help us ensure that all of our meetings are as productive and effective as they can be. Every single time we meet, we keep these 10 principles at the top of our minds. Our meeting mantras are perfect for us, but your meeting culture may call for some tweaks, or maybe even completely different mantras. These are a few of ours; take them for your team or use them as a springboard to create your own meeting mantras.

We've dug into many of our meeting mantras already.

→ **No purpose, no meeting:** If you don't have a clear purpose, don't call a meeting

→ **Disagree and commit:** Not everyone has to agree to come to a consensus

→ **Do the work in the meeting:** Bring a prototype or idea to flesh out and explore, not just to talk about

→ **Capture room intelligence:** The collective is smarter and more innovative than any individual

→ **Embrace the child's mind:** Be present, playful and curious

→ **Respect everyone's time:** Construct a detailed agenda and stick to it

→ **Debrief for durability:** Assign tasks for after the meeting is over and remind everyone of the big takeaways

→ **Bring your best self:** Team members who choose to attend your meeting are going to bring their best selves

→ **Foster emotional safety:** Take the time to ask each person how they are feeling and actively include everyone in attendance

→ **Decide what not to do:** Use your meetings as an opportunity to commit to having fewer things to do

These mantras are at the core of everything we've explored so far. Incorporating some or all of these mantras will help you develop good meeting habits; they will make you more intentional about the design of your meeting systems and take control of your meeting culture.

> Maybe some of these mantras aren't worded correctly for your team. Create your own!

This is a great time to utilize the human-centered design process above.

Think about what your perfect meeting culture looks like and create mantras that will help you achieve it.

Consider how your meeting mantras intersect with each other and focus on mantras that help guide what your team will do, not what they won't do.

Create a list of mantras that will serve as a checklist for your team to achieve the meeting culture that will best serve them.

CHAPTER SUMMARY
KEY TAKEAWAYS:

- Consider workshopping a better meeting culture with your team and fellow leaders.

- A lesson isn't learned until you have addressed it.

- Audit your meeting systems and look for debt.

- Smaller teams = less FOMO.

- Design your own meeting mantras.

CHAPTER 10

How Meetings Will Evolve

Facilitation has always mattered, but as the workplace faces more and more frequent change in the face of technological advancement, its importance will continue to grow. The nature of work is changing, and we must pay attention to the shifting landscape.

10.1   Change Is Always Coming

At this point, the only way for organizations to outpace a growing snowball of technological advancement is to be highly adaptive. What's more, these constant changes result in quick shifts in cultural notions surrounding workplace culture and employee expectations. Change isn't just coming; it's already here.

Perhaps one of the largest and most transformative changes we've recently seen in office culture is the shift from hierarchical leadership to distributed leadership.

In hierarchical leadership models, there are rigid structures of power—big bosses who call all the shots and large numbers of less autonomous team members at the bottom who defer to the decisions and desires of those above them.

There are many pitfalls to this approach to leadership. Utilizing room intelligence is nearly impossible, as team members are not encouraged to contribute, but instead only to complete a list of tasks. Less experienced team members will rarely get the opportunity to learn from more experienced team members. Arguably worst of all, the weight of every idea and decision falls on one person—one single manager who, no matter how incredible, is not as capable, well-rounded, creative, or experienced as an entire team of people with unique skill sets, capabilities and insights.

> Design multi-layered, interwoven networks of leadership so you can adapt to changes with more grace.

Adaptive organizations have replaced hierarchical leadership with distributed leadership and bottom-up project management. In a distributed leadership structure, team members within a group are specialists in their own work. They are empowered to act independently and trusted to ask for help when they need it rather than being constantly supervised. Teams make decisions through magical meetings and come to a consensus (sometimes with the help of an outside facilitator) rather than operating within the limitations of a rigid hierarchical pyramid.

Their magical meetings then lead to bottom-up project management, where each team member actively takes part in the shaping of all of their projects. Tasks and deadlines are set according to team member input.

The respect for and reliance on the capabilities of each member of the team seen in this leadership style lead to more magical meetings and happier employees who take ownership over their work.

10.2 Why Modern Leaders Need to Be Facilitators and Coaches

Once upon a time, quantitative metrics reigned supreme in the workplace. All that mattered was each employee's numbers. The big boss at the top of the rigid leadership pyramid came up with all of the ideas, then took credit for their implementation by lower-level employees. More and more companies are moving away from this approach, and it will be flat-out archaic in the near future. As more work becomes automated, it is even more critical to focus on what makes humans special.

> Facilitators help organizations harness these uniquely human capabilities by coaching rather than managing.

Leaders with a facilitator's mindset ensure that everyone on the team has a voice, and when everyone has a voice, everyone has a personal stake in the work they're doing. People want to do meaningful work. If you aren't coaching your team members—nurturing their capabilities, harnessing their strengths, valuing their insights—they will go elsewhere.

> Adopting a facilitation mindset is important for retaining talent.

Soft skills—communication, creativity, problem-solving, etc.—are becoming more and more crucial to employee success as technology advances our ability to fill our individual gaps in hard-skill knowledge. Soft skills make team members adaptable—a crucial key to success as technology advances so rapidly. Hard skills are teachable; soft skills are coachable. To succeed in this age of technology, teams need to be coached. They need to be facilitated.

10.3 The Butterfly Effect: The healthy cycle of good facilitators and good participants

Here's the big secret about magical meetings: They're not just about the meetings themselves. When an organization creates a meeting culture that allows its teams to effectively collaborate and communicate, they will carry those skills and attitudes into everything they do. Innovation, creativity, adaptability, and communication will leak out of the meeting room and spill over into other projects, assignments, and meetings.

Facilitators model behavior they want to encourage in participants. In the moment, they may be focusing on helping the group perform a task, but in the big picture what they're doing is training participants to adapt to collaborative co-creation, rapid discovery, and inclusive decision-making.

Seed behaviors you hope to see. ←

Facilitators help everyone in the room bring out their potential; this will lead to team members discovering their teammates' strengths and capabilities, in turn creating better teamwork and a more inclusive environment outside of the meeting room.

Facilitators generate energy, engage the imagination, and build ownership over the project at hand. They turn conflict into a conduit for creativity, reframing discord as opportunity. They bring people together and foster enthusiasm.

> Truly great facilitation doesn't just result in a successful meeting; it transforms your organization with better habits and mindsets.

10.4 When to Hire a Facilitator (And What to Look For)

Facilitators are a powerful tool for your organization's meetings. Like any powerful tool, in some situations they can be overkill. So how do you decide when you should hire a facilitator?

Hiring a facilitator is a no-brainer when your meeting needs an unbiased leader. If the leadership at your organization—the person who would normally spearhead a meeting—has a personal or professional stake that may jeopardize outcomes, an unbiased facilitator should be brought in. Facilitators are neutral leaders; their only skin in the game is ensuring that the team sticks to the ground rules, stays on task, and actively participates. They are not involved in office politics and are therefore able to enforce the ground rules without confusion around their intent. Bringing a facilitator into these meetings also allows leadership to focus on active participation as a stakeholder without the added responsibilities of managing the meeting.

Because of their neutrality, facilitators can make team members feel more comfortable sharing unpopular ideas or unique opinions. The facilitator isn't invested in the content of the meeting, but rather the meeting's success, so they can skillfully navigate a politically or emotionally charged conversation. If you anticipate handling sensitive content during your meeting, it may be best to hire a facilitator.

Bring process instead of content. ←

Bringing in a facilitator can also be an awesome way to reset your meeting culture. If you've received a lot of negative feedback or if there's a general disenchantment about your organization's meeting culture, inviting a facilitator into the space can lower everyone's guard and improve the room's attitude. If you're already working to improve your organization's meetings, bringing in a facilitator can start your team off on the right foot.

New faces generate excitement and will take the team off autopilot if they're accustomed to meetings that are less than participatory. Because the team doesn't know the facilitator, they won't feel pressured to impress them as they might a supervisor. Therefore, bringing in an outside facilitator will often result in more candid conversation and enhance the flow of ideas in your meetings. If your organization has been stuck on an endeavor, an outside facilitator may be exactly what it needs to move forward.

Finally, hiring a facilitator may be a great learning tool. It can be overwhelming to make substantial changes to a long-established meeting system. If you like to learn by watching, observing a facilitator working with your team can be a valuable experience. You may even make discoveries about individual team members, as well as the team as a whole. Facilitators are experts at balancing personality types and leveling the metaphorical volume of voices in the room; watching a facilitator unlock the potential in all your team members will help you harness your team's capabilities.

You likely need a facilitator for a gathering that is high stakes, handles sensitive or controversial content, tackles a complex situation involving leaderships' opinions, or revolves around something that you've met about multiple times without getting anywhere. You may also want to bring in a facilitator to hit the reset button on your team's attitude toward meetings and to give you, as the team's future facilitator, a valuable learning experience.

Clearly, facilitators are secret weapons in a wide variety of situations. Not every meeting, however, requires one. When should you not bring in a facilitator?

Not every meeting needs an external facilitator. →

It is very unlikely that you need to hire a professional facilitator for a weekly team meeting. If your team meets regularly to share updates and ask questions, there is really no need to bring in a facilitator. Not only would these kinds of meetings not need the facilitators' large toolkit of frameworks, methods and expertise, but hiring someone else to run them would waste an opportunity for your organization's leadership to practice facilitation skills. Use these meetings as a chance to practice balancing participation, staying on schedule, and other facilitation skills we've discussed so far.

Not all meetings are high stakes.

> If your organization needs to make a low-stakes decision, a facilitator is not necessary and may even slow down the decision-making process.

There's no need to bring in an unfamiliar face to make a decision about employee birthday traditions or the office's snack list (unless things get really heated over what to purchase!).

Finally, logistical meetings may not need an outside facilitator. If your team is already on the same page about the big-picture aspects of what they're working on but needs to touch base on the finer, more technical details—such as updating the task list or locking down a date—you should not need to hire a facilitator. In some instances, these logistical decisions may be high stakes, but often small details of this nature just need to be nailed down quickly and informally. If your team spends 20 minutes discussing every small technicality of a project, the project will never be finished. Save outside facilitation for meetings that would really benefit from creative problem-solving, ideation, collaboration and unbiased leadership.

To help you figure out whether your upcoming meeting or workshop would benefit from an internal or external facilitator, we have created an assessment.

VISIT ONLINE RESOURCES TO
Download the assessment at www.magicalmeetings.com.

CHAPTER SUMMARY
KEY TAKEAWAYS:

- Great facilitators influence great participants, who influence great facilitators.

- All modern leaders are facilitators.

- Outside facilitators are ideal for high-stakes discussion and workshops.

- Magical meetings can lead to cultural transformation.

CHAPTER 11

Facilitation Strategies for the Future of Work

After transitioning ourselves and others into leading magical meetings during a global pandemic, we feel like we have been fast-forwarded into the future of facilitation. Tools and methods that might have seemed 30 years out now feel more like only five years away. As meeting geeks, we talk about these future states on a weekly basis, so we wanted to end by sharing our vision of what facilitation will look like in the future of work, thanks to technology we have been tinkering with lately.

11.1 Meeting Automations and Efficiencies

Have you ever been tasked with keeping meeting notes? It is a tedious process we don't wish on anyone. Most of us don't have a stenographer in our meetings, nor would we expect someone in the meeting to type out every word spoken, although having a transcript of the meeting is useful. Thanks to advances in artificial intelligence, there are applications that allow you to record your meeting dialog and have a fairly accurate transcript of the meeting afterward.

AI is also helping with attention management. Sometimes we can't have all participants in the room. And it's difficult to be engaged with a room if you are a virtual participant.

With AI-driven cameras, virtual participants have a panoramic view of the entire room with frequently updated camera angles based on who is speaking. This improves attention management for the virtual participant, and those of us meeting in person don't have to worry about setting up and configuring software for multiple cameras.

Case Study

The Potential of AI to Assist With Understanding Cultural Dynamics:

"One of the things we've all experienced in the recent acceleration of video meetings is how difficult it can be to 'read the room' (or read the Zoom call!) in a virtual meeting vs. in-person. Humans are not accustomed to interacting this way, especially for sustained periods of time.

"I would expect to see some major developments in AI to help lessen the cognitive and emotional load of virtual meetings, including behavioral data— who is getting heated? Quiet? Engaged vs. unengaged? For verbal and nonverbal communication analysis, this would feed real-time insights to participants with queuing, notifications and retrospectives on each meeting.

"This information will also help teams better understand real-time cultural dynamics to support diversity and inclusion. Along the same lines, there will be a movement to harness data gathered not only in meetings, but combined with participant surveying, calendar and data mining on post-meeting actions, and even wearables to monitor the biological impact of meetings, helping workers not only receive input, but also self-monitor in innovative ways."

Nicole Baer, Global Head of Marketing @Logitech

> The robots will take away the tedious parts of meetings and create room for more playtime in our magical meetings.

So rather than trying to facilitate a meeting and capture as much detailed structured data as possible, we can hand over that possibility to new technologies, allowing facilitators to be more present and hold space for our participants. If you have not heard of or used any automations similar to the ones we mention above, we highly recommend you get ahead of the curve and tinker with them now. The tools ultimately may not work for you, but at least interacting with them will give you a glimpse into the trends of tomorrow.

You can find an ongoing curated list of other amazing meeting automation tools on our website, www.magicalmeetings.com.

11.2 Five Ways Automation Technology Could Enhance Your Meetings

AI will continue to improve our meetings. Here are five predictions for how we will eventually include an AI as a participant in our workshops. We believe we will be able to do this sooner than you think, so keep these in mind for your own strategies for leveraging AI.

AI COULD HELP US CURATE CONCEPTS

Rather than be at a loss of ideas, we can leverage machine-learning algorithms (like the ones currently used in the visual curation platform Pinterest) to instantly curate visual mood boards in a concepting meeting. Participants can then consider and respond to these curated ideas rather than struggle with coming up with concepts from scratch.

AI COULD HELP US RUN SCENARIO SIMULATIONS

Instead of endless debate in a meeting on how things might turn out in the future, we can leverage predictive analytics to run multiple simulations of possible outcomes. Combine that with our breakthroughs in augmented-reality technology and you get what futurist Kevin Kelly calls "the Mirrorworld."[5] With our ability to rapidly create scenarios, Kelly says, "These scroll-forward scenarios will have the heft of reality because they will be derived from a full-scale present world. In this way, the mirrorworld may be best referred to as a 4-D world." Having this ability in meetings would allow us to fast forward into the future of what could manifest in an immersive way—adding an entirely new layer to decision-making.

AI COULD HELP US RESOLVE DISPUTES

We all know the person in the meeting who says, "That will never work," or the one who refuses to budge from their viewpoint. But thanks to advances in data hygiene and semantic learning, we will eventually leverage an AI real-time "fact checker" to quickly check somebody's claims. This will give the facilitator the means to have a more neutral, truthful meeting and prevent strong personalities from hijacking the meeting.

AI COULD HELP US DEVELOP A MORE REALISTIC ACTION PLAN

After a magical meeting there is a solid action plan. We must coordinate schedules, develop deadlines that are realistic, and let others know about the new action plan. This is a lot for one human or a group of humans to manage in short order. We predict a meeting follow-up AI agent that can scan the proposed action plan and give recommendations for more realistic deadlines given schedule conflicts, capacity constraints, and resource availability. These capabilities will be our sanity checks to make sure we don't under- or overcommit.

AI COULD ASSIST WITH WEIGHTED VOTING

Instead of equal voting on an issue in a meeting, we will leverage data and context analysis to make decisions. For a given topic in a specific domain, certain people with expertise in that domain would be weighted more heavily. Ray Dalio has already implemented this at his firm, Bridgewater. He says, "It is far better to weight the opinions of more capable decision makers more heavily than those of less capable decision makers. This is what we mean by 'believability weighting.' So how do you determine who is capable of what? The most believable opinions are those of people who 1) have repeatedly and successfully accomplished the thing in question, and 2) have demonstrated that they can logically explain the cause/effect relationships behind their conclusions. When believability weighting is done correctly and consistently, it is the fairest and the most effective decision-making system. It not only produces the best outcomes but also preserves alignment, since even people who disagree with the decision will be able to get behind it."[6] This kind of AI meeting participant will allow us to get more intelligent with our decision-making moments based on competency, experience and context.

AI will help us prioritize possibility over feasibility.

We have no doubt that we will incorporate the AI capabilities above into our magical meetings one day.

Right now, our advice to facilitators is to start experimenting with tools to help you curate concepts, develop action plans and make decisions in a smarter way. Eventually there will be AI technology helping you with it, so you might as well start experimenting with the delegation.

11.3 Crowdsourced Collaboration

Are you currently co-creating with outsiders, such as your industry partners and customers? It isn't only energizing to have non-obvious participants show up in our meetings, but they help us see beyond our blinders. Co-creation is essential for exceptional outcomes but, like everything else, it is evolving thanks to the internet.

We are seeing feedback and value-measurement platforms such as ProductHunt that enable entrepreneurs to get more clarity on their business ideas and value propositions.

Software pioneers are now using Twitter as an asynchronous forum to poll their followers on feature and pricing preferences.

You could argue that "subreddits" on the platform Reddit are asynchronous meetings with many crowdsourced ideas and the subreddit editor as the facilitator.

> Rather than only having magical meetings with our own team members, we will increasingly include outside perspectives.

The Design Sprint is a design-thinking workshop documented in the book *Sprint* by Jake Knapp that embodies learning from outsiders. So does our lightweight prototyping process The Design Dash. At the end of these discovery workshops, we showcase a prototype to outsiders and their feedback changes the course of our project.

Case Study

How a Supply Chain Technology Firm Leverages "Co-Innovation."

"At Kinaxis, we work on designing solutions for complex supply chain problems. This requires a significant amount of effort to be spent on the discovery and definition phases.

"We've embraced a spirit of 'co-innovation', collaborating with outside stakeholders, including customers, partners and domain experts, in design thinking workshops. The activities in these workshops are customized to meet the objectives of the design phase we're in.

"External participants in these workshops bring an important outsider perspective that sparks innovative thinking within the team,

influencing direction and outcomes. This approach also creates buy-in, lowers risk and accelerates our innovation process."

Matt Chmiel, Director, User Experience @ Kinaxis

Bringing in outsiders into your meeting will help you learn faster while also keeping you grounded in reality.

We imagine an eventual marketplace of experts and specialists who you can easily recruit to attend your meeting and help all attendees gain a fresh perspective.

What outsiders could you invite to your next workshop or meeting to help your team get out of their own biases? Reach out to them now and start the healthy habit of bringing in outside perspectives.

11.4   Adaptive Communication Systems

When the COVID-19 pandemic hit, we noticed what felt like five years of acceleration in virtual meetings within just a few weeks. We had to adapt quickly to keep meeting and working, so investing in more adaptive communication is a solid strategy for preparing for the unknown.

> As technology and culture evolve, so should our communication styles.

Two adaptive communication systems now have become our standards for communicating better.

Loom is a software tool helping teams replace long, confusing emails with more quickly digestible video screen shares with support for contextual commentary. Recipients of the video can respond to specific parts of the video with reactions and comments. This helps people share a visual message that sets context, which usually gets lost or misinterpreted via text. Rather than sending a long email to your workshop participants, you can now quickly produce an engaging video overview of your work and allow follow-up clarifying questions.

MURAL is a virtual whiteboard that allows people to create stickies, share inspiring photos, vote on decisions, and use other visual collaboration tools. We've found that a virtual whiteboard is most powerful when everyone is adding content in parallel. This multithreaded interaction means that everyone is adding their own nuanced perspective in real time, allowing us to move faster and go deeper than if we were waiting for each person to take their turn speaking.

These tools enable you to surface information visually to all participants rather than requiring them to intentionally seek it out. In a way, you are letting each person become a facilitator, allowing you to sit back and be the lazy facilitator.

| 11.5 | **Killing the Word "Meeting"** |

This is a bit contradictory given the title of this book, but we feel that the word "meeting" is flawed, and we hope that future teams upgrade their meeting taxonomy with more specific terms that better convey their purpose.

> Just replacing the word "meeting" in your event invite will help clarify your purpose.

Most meetings suck because they end up just being a status update that should have been asynchronous. When we are more specific, it becomes obvious whether the meeting is worthwhile and who needs to attend.

Replace the word "Meeting" with
[what you are doing] Workshop
[what you are creating] Creation Session
[what you are deciding] Decision Jam
Team-Building Activities
Prototype Review
Discuss Lessons Identified
Pivot or Persevere Decision Workshop

One of our long-time meeting mantras is "Do the work in the meeting." This concept of doing the work in the meeting isn't new. At the design consultancy IDEO, they've long talked about something called "Boyle's Law." Named for Dennis Boyle—an IDEO engineer with more than 50 patents—the law states that you should "Never attend a meeting without a prototype."

Allan Chochinov, chair of the School of Visual Arts MFA Products of Design, also wrote about his hatred of meetings and even created a Chrome and Slack extension that automatically changes the word "meeting" to "review" when you try to book an event.

This behavior of setting intentional titles in our calendar prevents us from just having a meeting where we semiupdate one other and instead coming to the meeting with something to review, make, or decide on —which in theory should lead to fewer meetings.

We have found that most meetings should have been a well-written update where people can comment whenever it is relevant and convenient for them.

Magical meetings are more like workshops filled with shorter moments of demonstration and decision-making.

We regularly set a "maker week" for our team. During that week, we have no meetings; we simply make/prototype. Then we have an artifact to share. When we do come together, we call it a workshop, review, decision, clarity circle, or facilitation practice—anything but a meeting.

11.6 Managers Become Facilitators

We once heard a joke that an engineer wanted to apply the Marie Kondo method (getting rid of things that don't spark joy) to their company and they got rid of all the managers!

Sometimes managers get a bad rap. They are often seen as people who get in the way. We have noticed, however, that the best managers are actually magical meeting facilitators in disguise. They manage a room of specialists and make progress with that room intelligence. They help catapult the work of makers rather than being seen as the people who slow things down with process.

> We imagine a future where all the great managers have replaced their titles with "facilitator."

Our definition of a facilitator is someone who makes things easier for everyone else. Imagine if all managers within a company practiced the non-obvious skills in this book.

In the age of automation, hosting and running meetings is essential for human work, and all managers have the opportunity to become Jedi facilitators. Once all managers become master facilitators, the meeting culture in a company transforms in ways that unlock the potential in everyone. This in turn will have a massive impact on the world.

CHAPTER SUMMARY
KEY TAKEAWAYS:

- Experiment with cutting-edge technologies before forming your opinion about them; they could be your next facilitator power move.

- Encourage all the managers you work with to act like facilitators.

- The word "meeting" has become obsolete as we upgrade our taxonomy to be more specific and intentional.

- Someone will step up to facilitate the AIs.

Meeting Science Fiction

We want to end this book with a bit of fiction that we believe is highly possible based on the patterns and trends we have observed while writing this book.

As sci-fi writer Frederik Pohl says, "The science fiction method is dissection and reconstruction. You look at the world around you, and you take it apart into all its components. Then you take some of those components, throw them away, and plug in different ones, start it up and see what happens. That's the method: restructure the world we live in in some way, then see what happens."

Or as renowned novelist and poet Ursula K. Le Guin puts it, "Science fiction is not to predict the future. Rather, it contemplates possible futures."

Science fiction can be used as a tool for helping companies better predict and plan for the future we may soon be operating in. In fact, there are new business strategy terms such as "design fiction" and "prototype fiction" emerging as practices where innovative companies are commissioning sci-fi authors to write imaginative stories about the company's future.[7]

So consider this conclusion our design fiction for you. We'll leave you with a few provocative glimpses into what meeting cultures might look like decades from now.

Imagine...

WE WILL DESIGN NEW MEETING WORLDS

We recently were given a demo of a virtual reality tool that allowed a group of futurists to have a conference on the moon. It was to scale, and you could teleport around and have a meeting within a virtual rendering of a building concept that an architect had dreamed up. That set and setting put everyone in a different mood. So what virtual worlds will you be creating in the future that don't require an expensive rocket ship ticket, but instead an approachable headset? You could create new worlds that make for a better design-thinking session or participatory decision-making workshop. Look no further than *Fortnite* to see this pattern emerging. The next generation is already rehearsing how to assemble new worlds and hosting ad hoc discussions on how to build a better world.

What world do you want to meet in? ➜

RATHER THAN FACILITATE TEAMS WITHIN COMPANIES, WE WILL FACILITATE CONSORTIUMS

As industries and value chains become more decentralized, industry patterns will have to collaborate and meet more effectively. Rather than having an annual consortium gathering, such meetings could happen weekly, and the facilitators of these consortiums will have to use all the futuristic tools mentioned in this book to manage the complexities of a consortium.

THE CREATIVE ECONOMY AND GIG ECONOMY IS GROWING, AND FACILITATION WILL BE A SUPER-POWER.

As the freelance economy grows, each of us needs to be part-entrepreneur, part-maker, and part-facilitator to make sure we are able to find the right gigs, collaborate with an exciting global remote marketplace, and facilitate change. If you are going to thrive in the creative economy, being a magical meeting facilitator will be as important for you as typing is for a freelance writer.

WE WILL ALL BECOME PROFESSIONAL GAMERS

As AI takes over the mundane parts of our virtual meetings, we now have more open space to be creative. We created an application called Control Room that allows virtual meeting participants to play simple games to generate great ideas while following many of the principles in this book. And we are seeing other virtual facilitation methods that look like professional arcade games. You don't want to be left out not knowing how to play these games or how to introduce them to other people. So find your own gaming hobby and get inspired by the idea of playing games as a professional!

SOME OF US WILL FACILITATE DIFFERENT AIs

This idea might seem wild, but it isn't as far off as you might think. Right now, most of our AI breakthroughs are with narrow AIs and companies equipped with their own narrow AI applications. Who is going to facilitate these AI agents when it is time for them to cooperate? What about two companies that are AI-driven deciding to merge? Who is going to facilitate the discussion that considers both human stakes and algorithms? Data literacy and AI literacy are going to be important parts of being credible facilitators for these kinds of scenarios.

> In all of these future states, the core principles in this guide will still matter, so start practicing now and help those around you learn these non-obvious meeting techniques so that they become obvious to all.

Endnotes

1. Sagan, Carl. *Pale Blue Dot*. p. 6-7. United States: Random House USA Inc.

2. Lipmanowicz, Henri & McCandless, Keith, *The Surprising Power of Liberating Structures: Simple Rules to Unleash a Culture of Innovation*, Liberating Structures Press (February 19, 2014)

3. Knapp, Jake. Zeratsky, John & Kowitz, Braden, *Sprint: How to Solve Big Problems and Test New Ideas in Just Five Days*, Simon and Schuster, 2016

4. Willink, J., & Babin, L. *Extreme Ownership: How U.S. Navy SEALs Lead and Win*. Second edition. p. 276. (2017). New York: St. Martin's Press.

5. Kelly, Kevin. "AR Will Spark The Next Big Tech Platform—Call It Mirrorworld." (February 12, 2019) Wired. Condé Nast Inc.. Fabric of Digital Life.

6. Dalio, Ray. *Principles: Life and Work*. First Simon & Schuster hardcover edition. p. 371. New York: Simon and Schuster, 2017.

7. Gunn, Eileen. "How America's Leading Science Fiction Authors Are Shaping Your Future." Smithsonian.com, Smithsonian Institution, 1 May 2014, https://www.smithsonianmag.com/arts-culture/how-americas-leading-science-fiction-authors-are-shaping-your-future-180951169/

Index

About the Authors

Douglas Ferguson is an entrepreneur and human-centered technologist. He is the founder and president of Voltage Control, an Austin-based change agency that helps enterprises spark, accelerate, and sustain innovation. He specializes in helping teams work better together through participatory decision making and design inspired facilitation techniques. He has helped transform teams from Nike, U.S. SOCOM, Google, the Air Force, Apple, Adobe, Dropbox, Fidelity, Vrbo, Liberty Mutual, Humana, and SAIC.

Douglas is a thought leader and master facilitator of Design Sprints, Innovation Acceleration, Team Alignment, Meeting Systems, Culture Transitions, and Change Transformations. He is also the author of three books: Beyond the Prototype, How to Remix Anything (co-authored), and Start Within (co-authored). He has been published in Forbes, Fast Company, Innovation Leader, and is a regular contributor to The Future Shapers. He publishes a weekly podcast called Control the Room.

Motivated by a mission to rid the world of horrible meetings and offer meaningful magical meetings in their place, Voltage Control is calling upon fellow facilitators to transform meeting and innovation culture. From free weekly community meetups to

Control the Room–the annual facilitator summit, Voltage Control is building a community of facilitators to change the world

Douglas is active in the Austin startup community where he serves on the board of several non-profits, mentors startups, and advises early-stage ventures. Prior to founding Voltage Control, Douglas held CTO positions at numerous Austin startups where he led product and engineering teams.

When not facilitating or coaching facilitators you might find Douglas patching up his Modular Synth, boxing, or doing pilates.

John Fitch is an entrepreneur and business coach that helps organizations become more calm and creative. He is co-author of the international bestseller Time Off: A Practical Guide to Building Your Rest Ethic and Finding Success Without the Stress, a book that expands our value of time off and how our rest and leisure are as important as our work. His ideas have been featured in Fast Company, Financial Times, Thrive Global, Entrepreneur Magazine, and other publications. He has empowered teams at Twitter, Gitlab, Baystate Health, and other forward-thinking companies embracing more creativity in the workplace.

John loves facilitating the art of connecting new dots to create narratives, products, and profitable businesses. When new ideas aren't successful, it's usually because the team was overconfident about if a customer would spend money on their idea. He specializes in quickly shipping an idea to see if the market will pay for it. It involves a lot of play, unlearning, empathy, and a keen focus on usefulness.

John was also an Entrepreneur in Residence at Animal Ventures. He coached Fortune 100 leadership on leading distributed software teams at the intersection of machine learning, robotics, and distributed computing during this time.

John is a proud graduate of Seth Godin's altMBA. He uses the experience to coach leaders on embracing tension, dancing with fear, making lean decisions, operating under ambiguity, understanding others' world-views, risk-taking, critical thinking, storytelling, driving innovation, securing buy-in, and making change happen.

Outside of coaching and writing, you can find John adventuring out in the wild, studying natural intelligence, and learning from landscapes.

Acknowledgments

We would like to thank you in advance for hosting or participating in the next magical meeting. The world needs us to gather, create, connect and change culture for the better. We can't do it alone.